The **E** Myth
Accountant

The **E**Myth Accountant

Why Most Accounting Practices Don't Work and What to Do About It

MICHAEL E. GERBER
M. DARREN ROOT

WILEY

John Wiley & Sons, Inc.

Published by John Wiley & Sons, Inc., Hoboken, New Jersey.

Published simultaneously in Canada.

For general information on our other products and services or for technical support, please contact our Customer Care Department within the United States at (800) 762-2974, outside the United States at (317) 572-3993 or fax (317) 572-4002.

Wiley also publishes its books in a variety of electronic formats. Some content that appears in print may not be available in electronic books. For more information about Wiley products, visit our web site at www.wiley.com.

ISBN 978-0-470-50366-9 (cloth); ISBN 978-1-118-00781-5 (ebk); ISBN 978-1-118-00782-2 (ebk); ISBN 978-1-118-00783-9 (ebk)

Printed in the United States of America

10 9 8 7 6 5 4 3 2 1

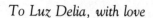

To Luz Delia, with love

CONTENTS

viii   Contents

A WORD ABOUT THIS BOOK

Michael E. Gerber

My first E-Myth book was published in 1985. It was called *The E-Myth: Why Most Small Businesses Don't Work and What to Do About It.*

Since that book's publication (and my creation of companies to provide business development services to its many readers), millions have read *The E-Myth* and the book that followed, *The E-Myth Revisited*, and tens of thousands have participated in our various E-Myth events, consulting, and aligned services.

Darren Root, coauthor of *The E-Myth Accountant*, is one of those more-than-enthusiastic readers. As a direct result of his enthusiasm, he has applied the E-Myth principles to the development of his accounting practice—to the point where it has risen to become a leader in its profession.

This book is the product of two things: my lifelong work conceiving, developing, and growing the E-Myth way into a business model that has been applied to every imaginable kind of company in the world, and Darren Root's extraordinary experience and success applying the E-Myth to his equally extraordinary accounting enterprise, Root & Associates, LLC.

So it was that one day, while sitting with my muse—which I think of as my inner voice, and which many who know me think of as "Here we go again!"—I thought about the creation of an entire series of E-Myth vertical books.

That series, of which this book is one of the first, would be coauthored by experts in every industry who had successfully applied my E-Myth principles to the extreme development of a practice—a very small company—with the intent of growing it nationwide, and even worldwide. This is what Darren Root had in mind as he began to discover the almost infinite range of opportunities provided by thinking the E-Myth way.

Upon seeing the possibilities of this new idea, I immediately went to Robert Armstrong and Sandy Fisch, two true E-Myth attorneys, and shared my excitement with them.

Not surprisingly, they said, "Let's do it!"

So, the first coauthored E-Myth book was born: *The E-Myth Attorney*.

And so, this book was born as well, when Darren first heard of the idea and said, with the very same entrepreneurial enthusiasm displayed by Robert and Sandy, "Yes, Michael, let's do it!"

And do it we did.

Welcome to one of the very first E-Myth vertical market expert books, *The E-Myth Accountant: Why Most Accounting Practices Don't Work and What to Do About It*.

Read it, enjoy it, and let us—Darren Root and I—help you apply the E-Myth point of view to the re-creation, development, and extreme growth of your accounting practice into an enterprise you can be justifiably proud of.

To your life, your wisdom, and the life and success of your clients—good reading.

—Michael E. Gerber
Chief Dreamer
Michael E. Gerber Partners
Carlsbad, California

A NOTE FROM
M. DARREN ROOT

s a practicing certified public accountant (CPA) for more than 25 years, I have an intimate knowledge of the obstacles accounting professionals face every day. In the absence of proper principles and planning, changing mandates, tax laws, technology, staffing, and client retention (and the list goes on) can add up to chaos and disaster. I've experienced firsthand the pain such chaos evokes. However, I've also experienced the feeling of tremendous relief brought about by implementing the E-Myth message in my firm. Having made the journey and done the work myself, I can say without pause that reading this book and adopting its message will transform the way you run your firm and, ultimately, your life.

It's been more than a decade since I adopted the principles set forth in Michael Gerber's *The E-Myth: Why Most Small Businesses Don't Work and What to Do About It*, but I can still remember the minute details of my journey from chaos to clarity. The moment of my great epiphany is what is most ingrained in my memory.

I had been in business for over 10 years. My firm was growing rapidly in both client base and staff. I found myself in a place all too familiar to many accounting professionals today: I was so busy working *in* my firm, that I had no time to work *on* it. I struggled to keep my head above water—taking on more and more clients, while giving up no responsibilities. And where did that get me? Enslaved to my own firm and estranged from my family—the exact opposite of what I had set out to create. I knew then that I had to make some significant changes.

I started my journey in the business section of my local bookstore. I picked up a copy of *The E-Myth* and was immediately engaged. I identified with the book's main "character," having experienced the same growing pains and feelings of insecurity related to implementing big changes. Deep into the book came the epiphany—the moment I realized that I had the power to mold the business I had originally set out to create—a well-structured firm that would yield significant revenue, while affording me true life–work balance.

Today, I still run my firm on the core principles described in *The E-Myth*. The E-Myth philosophy enabled me to recalibrate my practice, successfully transitioning from the traditional and antiquated way of doing business into what I've termed a Next Generation Accounting Firm™. Next-generation firms have opened their minds to a new way of doing business—that is, they've adopted appropriate technologies and practices to support highly efficient processes that yield higher profits and demand far less time investment. By applying the same principles, I've been able to build a nationally recognized organization that has educated hundreds of accountants about how to leverage their technical acumen and leadership skills to build highly efficient, money-making practices.

Perhaps the most wonderful aspect of the E-Myth perspective is the ability to apply it universally. One definitive fact about the accounting profession that I've learned over the years is that, at the core, all firms are exactly alike. From an operational standpoint, no matter the services offered or the size of the entity, any firm can apply E-Myth principles and achieve the same results that I have. And I'm not simply speculating; I've witnessed the transformation of many firms.

I'm no idealist to believe that most accounting firms will accept this notion without question and suspicion. In fact, I've heard just about every excuse explaining why these principles are not a good fit. That's the old-school accounting profession mind-set. To truly benefit from this book, professionals have to reboot their thinking . . . be open to the idea of building a business and *not* just having a job. Old-school thinking will only keep accountants in the daily grind, or as Michael Gerber says, "doing it, doing it, doing it."

The fact is that we are part of a noble, honest, and well-respected profession. And I would bet that most of us started out with great passion and a dream to run our own successful firms. I would also bet that, for most, the reality is long hours, a fair amount of stress, and less-than-attractive profits. It's time to change that.

Many years ago I was fortunate enough to have my epiphany, which came from reading *The E-Myth*. Today, with many years of experience as both an accounting technician and transformational business leader, I now have the honor of coauthoring a book that can help you transform your firm into a highly efficient, profitable organization. Start by clearing your head of outdated concepts and open yourself up to a new way of operating your practice. I can only hope that this book will have the significant impact on you that the original *The E-Myth* had on me so many years ago.

—M. Darren Root, CPA.CITP
President, Root & Associates, LLC
CEO RootWorks, LLC
Executive Editor,
The CPA Technology Advisor

PREFACE

I am not an accountant, although I have helped dozens of accountants reinvent their accounting practices over the past 35 years.

I like to think of myself as a thinker, maybe even a dreamer. Yes, I like to *do* things. But before I jump in and get my hands dirty, I prefer to think through what I'm going to do and figure out the best way to do it. I imagine the impossible, dream big, and then try to figure out how the impossible can become the possible. After that, it's about how to turn the possible into reality.

Over the years, I've made it my business to study how things work and how people work—specifically, how things and people work best together to produce optimum results. That means creating an organization that can do great things and achieve more than any other organization can.

The end product has been a series of books I've authored— *The E-Myth* books—as well as a company, E-Myth Worldwide, which I founded in 1977. For more than 30 years, E-Myth Worldwide has helped thousands of small-business owners, including many accountants, reinvent the way they do business by (1) rethinking the purpose of their accounting practice and (2) imagining how it could fulfill that purpose in innovative ways.

This book is about how to produce the best results as a real-world accountant in the development, expansion, and liberation of your practice. In the process, you will come to understand what the practice of accounting—as a *business*—is and what it isn't. If you keep focusing on what it isn't, you're destined for failure. But if you turn your sights on what it *is*, the tide will turn.

This book, intentionally small, is about big ideas. The topics we'll be discussing in this book are the very issues that accountants face daily in their practice. You know what they are: money, management, clients, and many more. My aim is to help you begin the exciting process of totally transforming the way you do business. As such, I'm confident that *The E-Myth Accountant* could well be the most important book on the practice of accounting as a business that you'll ever read.

Unlike other books on the market, this book's goal is not to tell you how to do the work you do. Instead, I want to share with you the E-Myth philosophy as a way to revolutionize the way you think about the work you do. I'm convinced that this new way of thinking is something accountants everywhere must adopt in order for their accounting practices to flourish during these trying times. I call it strategic thinking, as opposed to tactical thinking.

In strategic thinking, also called systems thinking, you, the accountant, will begin to think about your entire practice—the broad scope of it—instead of focusing on its individual parts. You will begin to see the end game (perhaps for the first time) rather than just the day-to-day routine that's consuming you—the endless, draining work I call "doing it, doing it, doing it."

Understanding strategic thinking will enable you to create a practice that becomes a successful business, with the potential to flourish as an even more successful enterprise. But in order for you to accomplish this, your practice, your business, and certainly your enterprise must work *apart* from you instead of *because* of you.

The E-Myth philosophy says that a highly successful account-ing practice can grow into a highly successful accounting business, which in turn can become the foundation for an inordinately successful accounting enterprise that runs smoothly and effi-ciently *without* the accountant having to be in the office for 10 hours a day, 6 days a week.

So what is "the E-Myth," exactly? The E-Myth is short for the entrepreneurial myth, which says that most businesses fail to fulfill their potential because most people starting their own business are not entrepreneurs at all. They're actually what I call *technicians suffering from an entrepreneurial seizure*. When technicians suffering from an entrepreneurial seizure start an accounting practice of their own, they almost always end up working themselves into a frenzy; their days are booked solid with appointments, one client after another. These accountants are burning the candle at both ends, fueled by too much coffee and too little sleep, and most of the time, they can't even stop to think.

In short, the E-Myth says that most accountants don't own a true business—most own a job. They're doing it, doing it, doing it, hoping like hell to get some time off, but never figuring out how to get their business to run without them. And if your business doesn't run well without you, what happens when you can't be in two places at once? Ultimately, your practice will fail.

There are a number of prestigious schools throughout the world dedicated to teaching the science of accounting. The problem is, they fail to teach the *business* of it. And because no one is being taught how to run their practice as a business, many accountants find themselves having to close their doors every year. You could be a world-class expert in tax planning, audit, financial-statement preparation, or bookkeeping, but when it comes to building a successful business, all that specified knowledge matters exactly zilch.

The good news is that you don't have to be among the statistics of failure in the accounting profession. The E-Myth philosophy I am about to share with you in this book has been successfully applied to hundreds of accounting practices just like yours with extraordinary results.

The key to transforming your practice—and your life—is to grasp the profound difference between going to work *on* your practice (systems thinker) and going to work *in* your practice (tactical thinker). In other words, it's the difference between going to work on your practice as an entrepreneur and going to work in your practice as an accountant.

The two are not mutually exclusive. In fact, they are essential to each other. The problem with most accounting practices is that the systems thinker—the entrepreneur—is completely absent. And so is the vision.

The E-Myth philosophy says that the key to transforming your practice into a successful enterprise is knowing how to transform yourself from a successful accounting technician into successful technician-manager-entrepreneur. In the process, everything you do in your accounting practice will be transformed. The door is then open to turning it into the kind of practice it should be—a practice, a business, an enterprise of pure joy.

The E-Myth not only *can* work for you but *will* work for you. In the process, it will give you an entirely new experience of your business and beyond. To your future and your life. Good reading.

—Michael E. Gerber

ACKNOWLEDGMENTS

M. Darren Root

Many heartfelt thanks to the entire RootWorks team for their dedication to educating and enhancing the accounting profession. I would particularly like to thank two of my business partners, J. Wade Schultz and Ryan Deckard—for without their support, I could not have chased my dreams.

Special thanks to my other business partner, Kristy Short Ed.D., for her unrelenting dedication to this project. And also for all the late-night and weekend hours spent editing this book and helping me effectively transition my thoughts to paper.

My deepest gratitude to my father, Morris D. Root, for passing on his wisdom and allowing me to work at his side during my early years as a CPA.

I would also like to thank each and every accounting professional that trusted me to guide them on their journey to becoming a Next Generation Accounting Firm™.

Heartfelt thanks also to my family for their support and never-ending understanding for the hours spent building my accounting firm, launching a consulting business, and then writing this book. To my wife, Michelle, who has been by my side and my best friend since we were teens. And to my kids, Andy, Meredith, and Alex, who I am so proud of and thankful for all you've taught me over the years.

And, finally, my gratitude to my faith, which has kept me strong through all that I do.

INTRODUCTION

A s I write this book, the recession continues to take its toll on American businesses. Like any other industry, accounting is not immune. Accountants all over the country are watching as clients defer or attempt to do their own tax preparation and financial planning. At a time when per capita disposable income is at an all-time low, many people are choosing not to spend their hard-earned money on accounting services for themselves or even for their companies. As a result, many clients are reducing accounting services to only those they consider essential, and regrettably, proper planning and improved practices become an expendable concern while industry revenue takes a sizeable dip into the red.

Faced with a struggling economy and fewer and fewer clients, many accountants I've met are currently asking themselves, "Why did I ever become an accountant in the first place?"

And it isn't just a money problem. After 35 years of working with small businesses, many of them accounting practices, I'm convinced that the dissatisfaction experienced by countless accountants is not just about money. To be frank, the recession doesn't deserve all the blame, either. Although the financial crisis our country is facing certainly hasn't made things any better, the problem started long before the economy tanked. Let's dig a little deeper. Let's go back to school.

Can you remember that far back? Whichever university or college you attended, you probably had some great teachers who helped you become the fine accountant you are. These schools excel at teaching the science of accounting; they'll teach you everything you need to know about general ledgers, tax codes, holding structures, and payroll. But what they *don't* teach is the consummate skill set needed to be a successful accountant, and they certainly don't teach what it takes to build a successful accounting enterprise.

Obviously, something is seriously wrong. The education that accounting professionals receive in school doesn't go far enough, deep enough, broad enough. Colleges and universities don't teach you how to relate to the *enterprise* of accounting or to the *business* of accounting; they only teach you how to relate to the *practice* of accounting. In other words, they merely teach you how to be an *effective* accountant, rather than a *successful* accountant.

That's why there are plenty of accountants who are effective, but very few who are successful. Although a successful accountant must be effective, an effective accountant does not have to be— and in most cases isn't—successful.

An effective accountant is capable of executing his or her duties with as much certainty and professionalism as possible.

A successful accountant, on the other hand, works balanced hours, has little stress, leads rich and rewarding relationships with friends and family, and has an economic life that is diverse, fulfilling, and shows a continuous return on investment.

A successful accountant finds time and ways to give back to the community, but at little cost to his or her sense of ease.

A successful accountant is a leader, someone who doesn't simply teach clients how to balance their books and pay their taxes, but a sage; a rich person (in the broadest sense of the word); a strong father, mother, wife, or husband; a friend, teacher, mentor, and spiritually grounded human being; a person who can see clearly into all aspects of what it means to lead a fulfilling life.

So let's go back to the original question: Why did you become an accountant? Were you striving just to be an effective one, or did you dream about real and resounding success?

I don't know how you've answered that question in the past, but I am confident that once you understand the strategic thinking laid out in this book, you will answer it differently in the future.

If the ideas here are going to be of value to you, it's critical that you begin to look at yourself in a different, more productive way. I am suggesting you go beyond the mere technical aspects of your daily job as an accountant and begin instead to think strategically about your accounting practice as both a business and an enterprise.

I often say that most *practices* don't work—the people who own them do. In other words, most accounting practices are jobs for the accountants who own them. Does this sound familiar? The accountant, overcome by an entrepreneurial seizure, has started his or her own practice, become his or her own boss, and now works for a lunatic!

The result: The accountant is running out of time, patience, and ultimately money. Not to mention paying the worst price anyone can pay for the inability to understand what a true practice is, what a true business is, and what a true enterprise is—the price of his or her life.

In this book I'm going to make the case for why you should think differently about what you do and why you do it. It isn't just the future of your accounting practice that hangs in the balance. It's the future of your life.

The E-Myth Accountant is an exciting departure from my other sole-authored books. In this book, M. Darren Root—a licensed CPA.CITP who has successfully applied the E-Myth to the development of his accounting practice—shares his secrets about how he achieved extraordinary results using the E-Myth paradigm. In addition to the time-tested E-Myth strategies and systems I'll be sharing with you, you'll benefit from the wisdom, guidance, and practical tips provided by an accountant who's been in your shoes.

The problems that afflict accounting practices today don't only exist in the field of accounting; the same problems are confronting every organization of every size, in every industry in every country in the world. *The E-Myth Accountant* is the second in a new series of E-Myth expert books that will serve as a launching pad for Michael E. Gerber Partners™ to bring a legacy of expertise to small, struggling businesses in *all* industries. This series will offer an exciting opportunity to understand and apply the significance of E-Myth methodology, in both theory and practice, to businesses in need of development and growth.

The E-Myth says that only by conducting your business in a truly innovative and independent way will you ever realize the unmatched joy that comes from creating a truly independent business, a business that works *without* you rather than *because* of you.

The E-Myth says that it is only by learning the difference between the work of a *business* and the business of *work* will accountants be freed from the predictable—and often overwhelming—tyranny of the unprofitable, unproductive routine that consumes them on a daily basis.

The E-Myth says that what will make the ultimate difference between the success or failure of your accounting practice is first and foremost how you *think* about your business, as opposed to how hard you work in it.

So, let's think it through together. Let's think about those things—work, clients, money, time—that dominate the world of accountants everywhere.

Let's talk about planning. About growth. About management. About getting a life!

Let's think about improving your and your family's life through the development of an extraordinary practice. About getting the life you've always dreamed of, but never thought you could actually have.

Envision the future you want, and the future is yours.

CHAPTER

1

The Story of Steve and Peggy

Michael E. Gerber

You leave home to seek your fortune and, when you get it, you go home and share it with your family.

—Anita Baker

Every business is a family business. To ignore this truth is to court disaster.

I don't care whether or not family members actually work in the business. Whatever their relationship with the business, every member of an accountant's family will be greatly affected by the decisions an accountant makes about the business. There's just no way around it.

1

Unfortunately, like most service professionals, accountants tend to compartmentalize their lives. They view their practice as a profession—what they do—and therefore it's none of their family's business.

"This has nothing to do with you," says the accountant to his wife, with blind conviction. "I leave work at the office and family at home."

And with equal conviction, I say, "Not true!"

In actuality, your family and your accounting practice are inextricably linked to each other. What's happening in your practice is also happening at home. Consider the following statements and ask yourself whether each is true:

- If you're angry at work, you're also angry at home.
- If you're out of control in your accounting practice, you're equally out of control at home.
- If you're having trouble with money in your practice, you're also having trouble with money at home.
- If you have communication problems in your practice, you're also having communication problems at home.
- If you don't trust in your practice, you don't trust at home.
- If you're secretive in your practice, you're equally secretive at home.

And you're paying a huge price for it!

The truth is that your practice and your family are one—and you're the link. Or you should be. Because if you try to keep your practice and your family apart, if your practice and your family are strangers, you will effectively create two separate worlds that can never wholeheartedly serve each other. Two worlds that split each other apart.

Let me tell you the story of Steve and Peggy Walsh.

The Walshes first met in college. Before long, they found themselves attending a cram session to study for the CPA exam,

Steve pursuing public accounting and Peggy auditing. When their project discussions started to wander beyond federal tax laws and cost accounting into their personal lives, they discovered they had a lot in common. By the end of the course, they weren't just talking in class; they were talking on the phone every night . . . and *not* about depreciation schedules.

Steve thought Peggy was absolutely brilliant, and Peggy considered Steve the most passionate man she knew. It wasn't long before they were engaged and planning their future together. A week after graduation, they were married in a lovely garden ceremony in Peggy's childhood home.

While the two completed their post-graduate studies, they worked hard to keep their finances afloat. They worked long hours and studied constantly; they were often exhausted and struggled to make ends meet. But through it all, they were committed to what they were doing and to each other.

After passing the CPA exam, Steve became an associate in a busy regional accounting firm; Peggy began working in a large, publicly held technology company. Soon afterward, the couple had their first son, and Peggy decided to take a leave of absence to be with him. Those were good years. Steve and Peggy loved each other very much, were active members in their church, participated in community organizations, and spent quality time together. The Walshes considered themselves one of the most fortunate families they knew.

But work became troublesome. Steve grew increasingly frustrated with the way the practice was run. "I want to go into business for myself," he announced one night at the dinner table. "I want to start my own practice."

Steve and Peggy spent many nights talking about the move. Was it something they could afford? Did Steve really have the business and marketing skills necessary to make an accounting practice a success? Were there enough clients to go around? What impact would such a move have on Peggy's career at the company to which she intended to return, on their lifestyle, their son, their relationship? They asked all the questions they thought they needed to answer before Steve went into business for himself . . . but they never really drew up a concrete plan.

Finally, tired of talking and confident he could handle whatever he might face, Steve committed to starting his own accounting practice. Because she loved and supported him, Peggy agreed, offering her own commitment to help in any way she could. So Steve quit his job, took out a second mortgage on their home, and leased a small office nearby.

In the beginning, things went well. A building boom had hit the town, and new families were pouring into the area. Steve had no trouble getting new clients. His practice expanded, quickly outgrowing his office.

Within a year, Steve had employed an office manager, Clarissa, to run the front desk and handle the administrative side of the business. He also hired a staff accountant, Tim, to handle the client work. Steve was ecstatic with the progress his young practice had made. He celebrated by taking his wife and son on vacation to Italy.

Of course, managing a business was more complicated and time-consuming than working for someone else. Not only did Steve supervise all the jobs Clarissa and Tim did, but he was continually looking for work to keep everyone busy. When he wasn't scanning journals of accounting publications to stay abreast of what was going on in the field or fulfilling continuing education requirements to stay current on the latest best practices, he was wading through client paperwork, or speaking with Internal Revenue Service (IRS) agents (which often degenerated into *arguing* with the IRS). He also found himself spending more and more time on the telephone dealing with client complaints and nurturing relationships.

As the months went by and more and more clients came through the door, Steve had to spend even more time just trying to keep his head above water.

By the end of its second year, the practice, now employing two full-time and two part-time people, had moved to a larger office downtown. The demands on Steve's time grew with the practice.

He began leaving home earlier in the morning, returning home later at night. He drank more. He rarely saw his son. For the most part, Steve was resigned to the problem. He saw the hard work as essential to building the "sweat equity" he had long heard about.

Money was also becoming a problem for Steve. Although the practice was growing like crazy, money always seemed scarce when it was really needed. He had discovered that many of his clients were often slow to pay, figuring that their accountant wasn't going to squawk. When they did pay, they often cut his fee.

When Steve had worked for somebody else, he had been paid twice a month. In his own practice, he often had to wait to get paid—sometimes for months. He was still owed money on client work he had completed more than 90 days before.

Complaints to late-paying clients fell on deaf ears. They would assure him that cash flow would improve and promise to do their best to budget a paydown of their obligation. Of course, no matter how slowly Steve got paid, he still had to pay *his* people. This became a relentless problem. Steve often felt like a juggler dancing on a tightrope. A fire burned in his stomach day and night.

To make matters worse, Steve began to feel that Peggy was insensitive to his troubles—not that he often talked to his wife about the practice. "Business is business" was Steve's mantra. "It's my responsibility to handle things at the office," he thought, "and Peggy's responsibility to take care of her own job and the family."

Peggy herself was working late hours at her firm, and they'd brought in a nanny to help with their son. Steve couldn't help but notice that his wife seemed resentful, and her apparent lack of understanding baffled him. Didn't she see that he had a practice to take care of? That he was doing it all for his family? Apparently not.

As time went on, Steve became even more consumed and frustrated by his practice. When he went off on his own, he remembered saying, "I don't like people telling me what to do." But people were *still* telling him what to do. On one particularly frustrating morning, his office had to get a last-minute pro forma out the door for a client acquisition. After holding for 25 minutes, Steve learned that his client had passed on the opportunity the previous day. Steve was furious, but he couldn't take out his upset on the client, or on his team, so he just bottled it up inside.

Not surprisingly, Peggy grew more frustrated by her husband's lack of communication. She cut back on her own hours at the firm to focus on their family, but her husband still never seemed to be around. Their relationship grew tense and strained. The rare moments they *were* together were more often than not peppered by long silences—a far cry from the heartfelt conversations that had characterized their relationship's early days when they'd talk into the wee hours of the morning.

Meanwhile, Tim, the staff accountant, was also becoming a problem for Steve. Tim never seemed to have the financial information Steve needed to make decisions about payroll, client work, and general operating expenses, let alone how much money was available for Steve and Peggy's living expenses.

When questioned, Tim would shift his gaze to his feet and say, "Listen, Steve, I've got a lot more to do around here than you can imagine. It'll take a little more time. Just don't press me, okay?"

Overwhelmed by his own work, Steve usually backed off. The last thing Steve wanted was to upset Tim and have to do the books himself. He could also empathize with what Tim was going through, given the practice's growth over the past year.

Late at night in his office, Steve would sometimes recall his first years out of school. He missed the simple life he and his family had shared. Then, as quickly as the thoughts came, they would vanish. He had work to do and no time for daydreaming. "Having my own practice is a great thing," he would remind himself. "I simply have to apply myself, as I did in school, and get on with the job. I have to work as hard as I always have when something needed to get done."

Steve began to live most of his life inside his head. He began to distrust his people. They never seemed to work hard enough or to care about his practice as much as he did. If he wanted to go get something done, he usually had to do it himself.

Then one day, the office manager, Clarissa, quit in a huff, frustrated by the amount of work that her boss was demanding of her. Steve was left with a desk full of papers and a telephone that wouldn't stop ringing.

Clueless about the work Clarissa had done, Steve was overwhelmed by having to pick up the pieces of a job he didn't understand. His world turned upside down. He felt like a stranger in his own practice.

Why had he been such a fool? Why hadn't he taken the time to learn what Clarissa did in the office? Why had he waited until now?

Ever the trouper, Steve plowed into Clarissa's job with everything he could muster. What he found shocked him. Clarissa's work space was a disaster area! Her desk drawers were a jumble of papers, coins, pens, pencils, rubber bands, envelopes, business cards, fee slips, eyedrops, and candy.

"What was she thinking?" Steve asked, astonished.

When he got home that night, even later than usual, he got into a shouting match with Peggy. He settled it by storming out of the house. Didn't anybody understand him? Didn't anybody care what he was going through?

He returned home only when he was sure Peggy was asleep. He slept on the couch and left early in the morning, before anyone was awake. He was in no mood for questions or arguments.

What lessons can we draw from Steve and Peggy's story? I've said it once and I'll say it again: *Every business is a family business*. Your business profoundly touches each member of your family, even if they never set foot inside your office. Every business either gives to the family or takes from the family, just as individual family members do.

If the business takes, the family is always first to pay the price.

In order for Steve to free himself from the prison he created, he would first have to admit his vulnerability. He would have to confess to himself and his family that he really doesn't know enough about his own practice and how to grow it.

Steve tried to do it all himself. Had he succeeded, had the practice supported his family in the style he imagined, he would have burst with pride. Instead, Steve unwittingly isolated himself, thereby achieving the exact opposite of what he sought.

He destroyed his life—and his family's life along with it.

Repeat after me: *Every business is a family business.*

Are you like Steve? I believe that all accountants share a common soul with him. You must learn that a business is only a business. It is not your life. But it is also true that your business can have a profoundly negative impact on your life unless you learn how to conduct it differently than most accountants do—and definitely differently than Steve did.

Steve's accounting practice could have served his and his family's life. But for that to happen, he would have had to learn how to master his practice in a way that was completely foreign to him.

Instead, Steve's practice consumed him. Because he lacked a true understanding of the essential strategic thinking that would have allowed him to create something unique, Steve and his family were doomed from day one.

This book contains the secrets that Steve should have known. If you follow in Steve's footsteps, prepare to have your life and business fall apart. But if you apply the principles we'll discuss here, you can avoid a similar fate.

Let's start with the subject of *money*. But, before we do, let's listen to the accountant's view of the story I just told you. Let's talk with Darren Root about how it's your story to write.

CHAPTER 2

This CPA's Personal Journey

M. Darren Root

If the ladder is not leaning against the right wall, every step we take just gets us to the wrong place faster.

—Steven R. Covey

When I graduated from college, I had my entire career ahead of me. Everything was my choice—where I headed and what goals I would accomplish. I was optimistic and hopeful that "the end" I had envisioned would eventually become a reality.

And what was that "end"? For me, it was an established, profitable accounting firm, with me at the helm. Operating my own firm would also offer other benefits, such as a flexible schedule and a healthy life–work balance. After all, how hard could that be to achieve?

Immediately after college, I joined a Big Four firm and gained the corporate experience I desired. From there, I went to work with my father, learning the ins and outs of the accounting profession through the small-firm lens. After a few years at the family business, I launched my own firm, convinced that I had reached the level of master technician and that my technical skill alone would be enough to run a successful firm.

Like most of my professional counterparts, I assumed that I was exempt from the trials of running a practice and that the learn-as-you-go method would suffice. I also labored under the misconception that technical skill alone would secure my success as a business owner. After a very short time, reality set in and I was faced with myriad issues that ranged from staffing to inadequate processes. And the more issues that emerged, the less prepared I was to deal with them. Soon, my time was consumed by managing problems and process defects, as well as slowing the spinning of my head. In the words of Michael Gerber, I was " . . . overcome by an entrepreneurial seizure."

The biggest heartache for me was that, although I had set out to own a business, all I'd accomplished was merely creating a job. I spent all my time working in my firm just to keep my head above water. I was so busy managing problems and completing client work that I was unable to emerge as a true leader. My dream of working for myself had translated into "working for a lunatic," as Michael Gerber says. I was my single biggest deterrent to making the transition from technician to savvy business leader. And let me tell you, they don't teach you how to do that transition in school.

The struggles I experienced are common and, unfortunately, are taking a toll on the profession at large. Although no definitive statistics are available, research has shown that accountants are predisposed to depression. Anecdotal evidence indicates that accounting professionals are often under a lot of pressure and work long hours to succeed. These elements contribute to a higher risk of depression.

Compound these elements with the pressures of an annual "busy season," and symptoms of depression can be exacerbated. During an average tax season, public accounting professionals work more than 10 hours a day for an extended period of time (Jones, Norman, & Weir 2010). During this period, accountants are faced with demanding and unforgiving deadlines, which can cause significant conflict with family and leave little to no time for leisure activity.

When you combine each of these stressors—long hours, an extended busy season, and limited time for family and leisure activities—you have the perfect recipe for job burnout. And burnout brings with it exclusively adverse consequences, affecting job performance and job satisfaction.

The hardest thing to admit is that no one sees it coming. I certainly didn't. So, when it hits, it hits hard, and you're left stunned and flailing to keep your head above water. Even worse, you find yourself working endless hours on tasks for which you have little passion or aptitude.

At some point, most accountants find themselves in a position of helplessness. We know things need to change, but we have no idea where to start. Eventually, some figure it out, like I did. But more often than not, accountants maintain the vicious cycle of working endless hours and seeing little gain. Just because this has been the way of the profession, however, does not mean we have to perpetuate the tradition.

How did we get here? How did the accounting profession become a mass of technicians and very few business leaders? These are the questions we will answer in this book. Read on, embrace the E-Myth philosophy, and discover how you can regain control of your practice and your life.

CHAPTER 3

On the Subject of Money

Michael E. Gerber

There are three faithful friends: an old wife, an old dog, and ready money.

—Benjamin Franklin

H ad Steve and Peggy first considered the subject of money, as we will here, their lives could have been radically different.

Money is on the tip of every accountant's tongue, on the edge (or at the very center) of every accountant's thoughts, intruding on every part of an accountant's life.

With money consuming so much energy, why do so few accountants handle it well? Why was Steve, like so many accountants, willing to entrust his financial affairs to a relative stranger? Why is money scarce for most accountants? Why is there less money than expected? And yet the demand for money is *always* greater than anticipated.

What is it about money that is so elusive, so complicated, so difficult to control? Why is it that every accountant I've ever met hates to deal with the subject of money? Why are they almost always too late in facing money problems? And why are they constantly obsessed with the desire for more of it?

Money—you can't live with it and you can't live without it. But you'd better understand it and get your people to understand it. Because until you do, money problems will eat your practice for lunch.

You don't need another accountant or a financial planner to do this. You simply need to prod your people to relate to money very personally. From the receptionist at the front counter to the newly hired junior accountant, they should all understand the financial impact of what they do every day in relationship to the practice's profit and loss.

And so you must teach your people to think like owners, not like technicians or office managers or receptionists. You must teach them to operate like personal profit centers, with a sense of how their work fits in with the practice as a whole.

You must involve everyone in the practice with the topic of money—how it works, where it goes, how much is left, and how much everybody gets at the end of the day. You also must teach them about the four kinds of money created by the practice.

The Four Kinds of Money

In the context of owning, operating, developing, and exiting from an accounting practice, money can be split into four distinct but highly integrated categories:

1. Income
2. Profit

3. Flow

4. Equity

Failure to distinguish how the four kinds of money play out in your practice is a surefire recipe for disaster.

Important Note: Even accountants and bookkeepers become confused about managing money. The information that follows comes from the real-life experiences of thousands of small-business owners—accountants included—most of whom were hopelessly confused about money when I met them. Once they understood and accepted the following principles, they developed a clarity about money that can only be called enlightened.

The First Kind of Money: Income

Income is the money accountants are paid by their practice for doing their job *in* the practice. It's what they get paid for going to work every day.

Clearly, if accountants didn't do their job, others would have to, and *they* would be paid the money the practice currently pays the accountants. Income, then, has nothing to do with *ownership*. Income is solely the province of *employeeship*.

That's why, to the accountant-as-*employee*, income is the most important form money can take. To the accountant-as-*owner*, however, it is the least important form money can take.

Most important; least important. Do you see the conflict? The conflict between the accountant-as-employee and the accountant-as-owner?

We'll deal with this conflict later. For now, just know that it is potentially the most paralyzing conflict in an accountant's life.

Failing to resolve this conflict will cripple you. Resolving it will set you free.

The Second Kind of Money: Profit

Profit is what's left over after an accounting practice has done its job effectively and efficiently. If there is no profit, the practice is doing something wrong.

However, just because the practice shows a profit does not mean it is necessarily doing all the right things in the right way. Instead, it just means that something was done right during or preceding the period in which the profit was earned.

The important issue here is whether the profit was intentional or accidental. If it happened by accident (as most profit does), don't take credit for it. You'll live to regret your impertinence.

If it happened intentionally, take all the credit you want. You've earned it. Because profit created intentionally, rather than by accident, is replicable—again and again. And your practice's ability to repeat its performance is the most critical ability it can have.

As you'll soon see, the value of money is a function of your practice's ability to produce it in predictable amounts at an above-average return on investment.

Profit can be understood only in the context of your practice's purpose, as opposed to *your* purpose as an accountant. Profit, then, fuels the forward motion of the practice that produces it. This is accomplished in four ways:

1. Profit is *investment capital* that feeds and supports growth.
2. Profit is *bonus capital* that rewards people for exceptional work.
3. Profit is *operating capital* that shores up money shortfalls.
4. Profit is *return-on-investment* capital that rewards you, the accountant-as-owner, for taking risks.

Without profit, an accounting practice cannot subsist, much less grow. Profit is the fuel of progress.

If a practice misuses or abuses profit, however, the penalty is much like having no profit at all. Imagine the plight of an accountant who has way too much return-on-investment capital and not enough investment capital, bonus capital, and operating capital. Can you see the imbalance this creates?

The Third Kind of Money: Flow

Flow is what money *does* in an accounting practice, as opposed to what money *is*. Whether the practice is large or small, money tends to move through it erratically, much like a pinball. One minute it's there; the next minute it's not.

Flow can be even more critical to a practice's survival than profit, because a practice can produce a profit and still be short of money. Has this ever happened to you? It's called "profit on paper," rather than in fact.

No matter how large your practice, if the money isn't there when it's needed, you're threatened—regardless of how much profit you've made. You can borrow it, of course. But money acquired in dire circumstances is almost always the most expensive kind of money you can get.

Knowing where the money is and where it will be when you need it is a critically important task of both the accountant-as-employee and the accountant-as-owner.

Rules of Flow

You will learn no more important lesson than the huge impact that flow can have on the health and survival of your accounting practice, let alone your business or enterprise. The following two rules will help you understand why this subject is so critical.

The first rule of flow states that your income statement is static, whereas the flow is dynamic.

Your income statement is a snapshot, whereas the flow is a moving picture. So, although your income statement is an excellent tool for analyzing your practice *after* the fact, it's a poor tool for managing it in the heat of the moment.

Your income statement tells you (1) how much money you're spending and where and (2) how much money you're receiving and from where.

Flow gives you the same information as the income statement, plus it tells you *when* you're spending and receiving money. In other words, flow is an income statement moving through time. And that is the key to understanding flow. It is about management in real time. How much is coming in? How much is going out? You'd like to know this daily, or even by the hour if possible. Never by the week or month.

You must be able to forecast flow. You must have a flow plan that helps you gain a clear vision of the money that's out there next month and the month after that. You must also pinpoint what your needs will be in the future.

Ultimately, however, when it comes to flow, the action is always in the moment. It's about *now*. The minute you start to meander away from the present, you'll miss the boat.

Unfortunately, few accountants pay any attention to flow until it dries up completely and slow pay becomes no pay. They are oblivious to this kind of detail until, say, clients announce that they won't pay for this or that. That gets an accountant's attention because the expenses keep on coming.

When it comes to flow, most accountants are flying by the proverbial seats of their pants. No matter how many people you hire to take care of your money, until you change the way you think about it, you will always be out of luck. No one can do this for you.

Managing flow takes attention to detail. But when flow is managed, your life takes on an incredible sheen. You're swimming with the current, not against it. You're in charge!

The second rule of flow states that money seldom moves as you expect it to.

But you do have the power to change that, provided you understand the two primary sources of money as it comes into and goes out of your accounting practice.

The truth is, the more control you have over the *source* of money, the more control you have over its flow. The sources of money are both inside and outside of your practice.

Money comes from *outside* your practice in the form of receivables, reimbursements, investments, and loans.

Money comes from *inside* your practice in the form of payables, taxes, capital investments, and payroll. These are the costs associated with attracting clients, delivering your services, operations, and so forth.

Few accountants see the money going *out* of their practice as a source of money, but it is.

When considering how to spend money in your practice, you can save—and therefore make—money in three ways:

1. Do it more effectively.
2. Do it more efficiently.
3. Stop doing it altogether.

By identifying the money sources inside and outside of your practice, and then applying these methods, you will be immeasurably better at controlling the flow in your practice

But what are these sources? They include how you do the following:

- Manage your services
- Buy supplies and equipment
- Compensate your people

- Plan people's use of time
- Determine the direct cost of your services
- Increase the number of clients
- Manage your work
- Collect reimbursements and receivables

And countless other tasks. In fact, every task performed in your practice (and ones you haven't yet learned how to perform) can be done more efficiently and effectively, dramatically reducing the cost of doing business. In the process, you will create more income, produce more profit, and balance the flow.

The Fourth Kind of Money: Equity

Sadly, few accountants fully appreciate the value of equity in their accounting practice. Yet, equity is the second most valuable asset any accountant will ever possess. (The first most valuable asset is, of course, your life. More on that later.)

Equity **is the financial value placed on your accounting practice by a prospective buyer.**

Thus, your *practice* is your most important product, not your services. That's because your practice has the power to set you free. That's right. Once you sell your practice—providing you get what you want for it—you're free!

Of course, to enhance your equity, to increase your practice's value, you have to build it right. You have to build a practice that works: a practice that can become a true business, and a business that can become a true enterprise. A practice/business/enterprise that can produce income, profit, flow, and equity better than any other accountant's practice can.

To accomplish that, your practice must be designed so that it can do what it does systematically and predictably—every single time.

The Story of McDonald's

Let me tell you the most unlikely story anyone has ever told you about the successful building of an accounting practice, business, and enterprise. Let me tell you the story of Ray Kroc.

You might be thinking, "What on earth does a hamburger stand have to do with my practice? I'm not in the hamburger business; I'm an accountant."

Yes, you are. But by practicing accounting as you have been taught, you've abandoned any chance to expand your reach, help more clients, or improve your services the way they must be improved if the practice of accounting—and your life—is going to be transformed.

In Ray Kroc's story lies the answer.

Ray Kroc called his first McDonald's restaurant "a little money machine." That's why thousands of franchisees bought it. And the reason it worked? Ray Kroc demanded consistency, so that a hamburger in Philadelphia would be an advertisement for one in Peoria. In fact, no matter where you bought a McDonald's hamburger in the 1950s, the meat patty was guaranteed to weigh exactly 1.6 ounces, with a diameter of $3^5/_8$ inches. It was in the McDonald's handbook.

Did Ray Kroc succeed? You know he did! And so can you, once you understand his methods. Consider just one part of Ray Kroc's story.

In 1954, Ray Kroc made his living selling the five-spindle Multimixer milkshake machine. He heard about a hamburger stand in San Bernardino, California, that had eight of his machines in operation, meaning it could make 40 shakes simultaneously. This he had to see.

Kroc flew from Chicago to Los Angeles and then drove 60 miles to San Bernardino. As he sat in his car outside Mac and Dick McDonald's restaurant, he watched as lunch customers lined up for bags of hamburgers.

In a revealing moment, Kroc approached a strawberry blonde in a yellow convertible. As he later described it, "It was not her sex appeal but the obvious relish with which she devoured the hamburger that made my pulse begin to hammer with excitement."

Passion.

In fact, it was the French fry that truly captured his heart. Before the 1950s, it was almost impossible to buy fries of consistent quality. Ray Kroc changed all that. "The French fry," he once wrote, "would become almost sacrosanct for me, its preparation a ritual to be followed religiously."

Passion and preparation.

The potatoes had to be just so—top-quality Idaho russets, 8 ounces apiece, deep-fried to a golden brown, and salted with a shaker that, as Kroc put it, kept going "like a Salvation Army girl's tambourine."

As Kroc soon learned, potatoes too high in water content— and even top-quality Idaho russets varied greatly in water content—will come out soggy when fried. And so Kroc sent out teams of workers, armed with hydrometers, to make sure all his suppliers were producing potatoes in the optimal solids range of 20 to 23 percent.

Preparation and passion. Passion and preparation. Look those words up in the dictionary, and you'll see Ray Kroc's picture. Can you envision your picture there?

Do you understand what Ray Kroc did? Do you see why he was able to sell thousands of franchises? Kroc knew the true value of equity, and, unlike Steve from our story, Kroc went to work *on* his business rather than *in* his business. He knew the hamburger wasn't his product—McDonald's was!

So what does *your* accounting practice need to do to become a little money machine? What is the passion that will drive you to build a practice that works—a turnkey system like Ray Kroc's?

Equity and the Turnkey System

What's a turnkey system? And why is it so valuable to you? To better understand it, let's look at another example of a turnkey system that worked to perfection: the recordings of Frank Sinatra.

Frank Sinatra's records were to him as McDonald's restaurants were to Ray Kroc. They were part of a turnkey system that allowed Sinatra to sing to millions of people without having to be there himself.

Sinatra's recordings were a dependable turnkey system that worked predictably, systematically, automatically, and effortlessly to produce the same results every single time—no matter where they were played, and no matter who was listening.

Regardless of where Frank Sinatra was, his records just kept on producing income, profit, flow, and equity, over and over . . . and they still do! Sinatra needed to produce only the prototype recording, and the system did the rest.

Kroc's McDonald's is another prototypical turnkey solution, addressing everything McDonald's needs to do in a basic, systematic way so that anyone properly trained by McDonald's can successfully reproduce the same results.

And this is where you'll realize your equity opportunity: in the way your practice does business, in the way your practice systematically does what you intend it to do, and in the development of your turnkey system—a system that works even in the hands of ordinary people (and accountants less experienced than you) to produce extraordinary results.

Remember:

- If you want to build vast equity in your practice, then go to work *on* your practice, building it into a business that works every single time.

- Go to work *on* your practice to build a totally integrated turnkey system that delivers exactly what you promised every single time.

- Go to work *on* your practice to package it and make it stand out from the accounting practices you see everywhere else.

Here is the most important idea you will ever hear about your practice and what it can potentially provide for you:

The value of your equity is directly proportional to how well your practice works. And how well your practice works is directly proportional to the effectiveness of the systems you have put into place upon which the operation of your practice depends.

Whether money takes the form of income, profit, flow, or equity, the amount of it—and how much of it stays with you—invariably boils down to this. Money, happiness, life—it all depends on how well your practice works. Not on your people, not on you, but on the system.

Your practice holds the secret to more money. Are you ready to learn how to find it?

Earlier in this chapter, I alerted you to the inevitable conflict between the accountant-as-employee and the accountant-as-owner. It's a battle between the part of you working *in* the practice and the part of you working *on* the practice. Between the part of you working for income and the part of you working for equity.

Here's how to resolve this conflict:

1. Be honest with yourself about whether you're filling *employee* shoes or *owner* shoes.

2. As your practice's key employee, determine the most effective way to do the job you're doing, *and then document that job*.

3. Once you've documented the job, create a strategy for replacing yourself with someone else (another accountant), who will then use your documented system exactly as you do.

4. Have your new employees manage the newly delegated system. Improve the system by quantifying its effectiveness over time.

5. Repeat this process throughout your practice wherever you catch yourself acting as employee rather than owner.

6. Learn to distinguish between ownership work and employeeship work every step of the way.

Master these methods, understand the difference between the four kinds of money, develop an interest in how money works in your practice . . . and then watch it flow in with the speed and efficiency of a perfectly delivered adjustment.

Now let's take another step in our strategic thinking process. Let's look at the subject of *planning*. But, first, let's listen to what Darren has to say about *money*.

CHAPTER 4

The Pursuit of Money

M. Darren Root

How am I going to live today in order to create the tomorrow I'm committed to?

—Anthony Robbins

Money, money, money . . . there never seems to be enough of it, and the majority of our time is spent in pursuit of it. At home we have mortgage and car payments, credit card debt, and college education expenses—all while trying our best to save for retirement (and hoping we can actually retire). At the office, we have rent, salaries, utilities, software, hardware, and the list goes on.

The fact is, the faster we grow our practices, the faster the cash wheel must turn to keep revenue flowing in. In terms of work and money, I think it's safe to assume that most accountants have felt like the proverbial hamster on a wheel.

Like most accounting professionals, I see many of our clients running the same race—hoping to earn and save enough to secure their future. The reality is, however, that most never achieve this goal. Occasionally I have a client who seems to be "winning." That is, this client lives comfortably, has plenty of money in a retirement account, and has mastered the art of balancing life and work. This is a rare breed of client, but when I see one, I take notice. And I ask myself, "What is this person doing differently?" After all, we are the accounting professionals, the money guys, so why can this goal be so elusive for us?

Living the good life is a wonderful pursuit and very attainable in our profession. But money alone will not provide us with the good life; only we can define the good life for ourselves. For me, the good life is having enough money to pay my bills, save for retirement, put my kids through college, build equity in my accounting firm, practice my faith, and thoroughly enjoy every day with my wonderful wife and kids. If I'm constantly working, all I might be able to accomplish is paying my bills and saving, while sacrificing my personal pursuits.

To obtain the life we desire, we must give up the idea that we are what we do. Our work should not define us. Rather, it should support the life we seek. The key is finding balance— true balance between our work and our personal lives. Yet, as we all know, mastering balance can be difficult . . . and at times, elusive.

During the past few years, I've traveled across the United States, talking with practitioners and listening to their challenges and successes. Based on extensive exposure to the profession, I've identified two common themes:

- First, I've learned that accountants are an incredibly wonder-ful group of people who care deeply about their clients' well-being and feel a deep sense of responsibility for their financial success.

• Oddly enough, the second thing that I've learned is in direct contrast with this observation. Although the profession as a whole cares a great deal for clients, most professionals harbor a deep-seated fear of losing clients and failing to attract new ones.

Neither mind-set is innately bad, until you apply either one to the business model. Because accountants care personally for their clients and tend to live in fear of failure (no matter how unsubstantiated that fear may be), the outcome is often mass client acquisition. Firms continue to take on clients, no matter whether they are a good fit for the firm, to ensure they are taken care of or to relieve the anxiety-related client attrition.

I've experienced the latter mind-set more often than not. What accountants fail to realize is that, in their pursuit of security, they are perpetuating a vicious circle—one that keeps them working, working, and working more *in* their firms and a fair distance from true life–work balance. Of course, this is never the intended outcome . . . just a cold, hard fact.

The goal in this chapter is to make accountants aware of this common mind-set, and then work to change it.

One of the incredible things that sets accounting apart from other professions is the nature of our work. Consider, for example, a law firm that specializes in divorce law. Once the divorce is handled, the client's account is closed. It's typically a one-time, all-inclusive fee—which is why a law firm has to work consistently to bring new clients in the door.

As accountants, we enjoy recurring business. Typically, clients are not a "one off." Each new client who signs up is an annuity to the firm. Whether that client is a daily, monthly, quarterly, or annual client, you can forecast to the day when that revenue will recur.

Think about it: recurring work and recurring revenue. It's the perfect model to develop a business because it allows accountants to define a desired client base, instead of taking on anyone who walks in the door. The real art of making money is not in the *quantity* of clients, but in the *quality* of clients.

Again, it's about changing the mind-set of how we grow our business and make an attractive profit. The biggest challenge is moving from technician to entrepreneur. We all enter the accounting profession because we have a technical skill, but most accountants will never make the transition from technician to business leader.

Please note that I'm not saying we should abandon our technical skills. The key point is that our efforts must be to transition to an entrepreneurial way of thinking.

The underlying purpose of this book is to help you make an honest assessment of your practice and decide whether you can separate your duties as an owner from your work as a technician. Just as Ray Kroc realized that his product wasn't hamburgers but the business that makes the hamburgers, practitioners must come to think of their accounting firms as the product. When you make that mental transition, you've taken the first step toward being the entrepreneur you planned to be when you started your firm.

Once you see your practice in this new way, you can then move into building your product—and the strategies and processes that will support a leading, next-generation firm.

Competency in business does not come naturally; it's a learned skill. We don't learn this skill in college. In fact, I don't recall a single course that discussed managing an accounting practice. Then, right out of college, many of us went on to work for an accounting firm that most likely operated on the premise of "doing it, doing it, doing it." The result: Our education and early learning provided us with little experience in creating the firm of our dreams. However, if you're willing to open your mind to a new way of thinking about how to create a successful accounting firm, this book will provide you with the tools you need.

Over the years, I also had to make the transition from working *in* my firm to working *on* my business. My journey led me to create a highly successful guide, "The Next Generation Accounting Firm." This guide provides clear steps for accountants who wish to transition from using old-school management tactics to becoming leaders of next-generation firms. It is from this guide that the core ideas in this book were developed.

The guide begins with creating a strategic vision. It asks you, as a firm leader, to take a step back, get away from the office, and spend a great deal of time thinking about what your ideal firm looks like. This includes the services offered, your role as leader, and the roles of others throughout the firm (receptionist, bookkeepers, staff accountants, and so on).

The next step is to write it all down—in other words, to be the architect of your firm. Once your vision is complete, you can begin to identify the proper strategies and processes to create a highly efficient, well-run firm.

Another important step to note is the necessity of communicating your firm's new strategic direction to staff and getting buy-in from each and every person involved. This is critical. You cannot expect to reengineer your entire firm without getting everyone on board from the beginning. After all, everyone will be affected by the change.

Let's step back a moment and look at what we've just discussed. Your firm can no longer be all things to all people. You first create a clear vision of where you want to go, and then you follow through with the proper supporting strategies and processes. You must also keep your staff in the loop at all times to maintain momentum and ensure change occurs. Ultimately, where you end up is a state of simple maintenance. Going forward, most of your time need be spent only on enhancing your business model, systems, and processes to ensure your firm continues to run like a well-oiled machine. At this point, you move from a technician working in your firm to a savvy business leader working on your product!

Once you know what you want your practice to look like, you need to take the time to develop your financial model. That is, how much money will it take to accomplish your goals? I find that whenever I can quantify something, I get peace of mind that I'm on track to execute my plan. First, define how much you want to make as your net profit for the firm—$200,000, $400,000, or more? It's your call. You know how much your practice can support and what your desired number is. Once you identify this number, you can work backward and figure out how many clients you need to support that number.

Forecasting a required client base is much easier than you might think. Earlier, I discussed how our profession is based on recurring revenue. That's one of the greatest things about what we do: the predictability of our revenue stream. We know on a month-to-month basis how much revenue will be generated—or at least we can forecast very close. From there, figure out the service mix that will drive your economic engine—that is, identify those services that you do best with a high level of efficiency.

Based on the predictability of workload and cash flow, you can now create incentives that will motivate your staff to meet goals. Consider bonuses for staff who exceed monthly or quarterly goals or perhaps base bonuses on profitability. Such incentives drive staff to scrutinize expenses more closely to assist in reaching revenue goals.

Accounting firms must understand the four kinds of money that Michael Gerber details in Chapter 3. After all, our profession deals with all four. It's a given that we all understand the concepts of income, profit, flow, and equity—but what most don't consider is how the relationships among these concepts create value in our practice.

Flow is important, but so is making a profit and maintaining appropriate funding to support daily operations. Many of us work with bankers every day on behalf of our clients. It makes sense to develop strong financial and lending relationships with banking contacts to help fund the firm during lower cash-flow periods. The goal I set for my firm is to have enough recurring revenue each month to fund monthly expenses, including my salary. During months when income is high, such as busy season, profits are put toward enhancing the business.

Michael also discusses Equity. The problem with many firms is that they don't consider Equity. This typically occurs because most accountants view their firms not as a business but as a job. As a result, they don't consider the value of the practice when it's time to retire. For many, their practice is potentially their biggest asset. Think about it . . . a well-run firm with recurring revenues that operates within a highly efficient system is often worth a lot of money. The very essence of a well-run business, commonly referred to as a "cash cow," is its ability to kick out cash and build equity. Those who can get their practices to that point realize the true value when it comes time to sell.

A few final thoughts . . . take the time to look at your practice under a powerful lens. Evaluate how it stacks up in terms of strategy, process, and the four kinds of money Michael discusses: income, profit, flow, and equity. Only then can you begin to develop the systems to move your practice forward.

CHAPTER 5

On the Subject of Planning

Michael E. Gerber

Luck is good planning, carefully executed.

—Anonymous

A nother obvious oversight revealed in Steve and Peggy's story was the absence of true planning.

Every accountant starting his or her own practice must have a plan. You should never begin to take on clients without a plan in place. But, like Steve, most accountants do exactly that.

An accountant lacking a vision is simply someone who goes to work every day. Someone who is just doing it, doing it, doing it. Busy, busy, busy. Maybe making money, maybe not. Maybe getting something out of life, maybe not. Taking chances without really taking control.

The plan tells anyone who needs to know *how we do things here*. The plan defines the objective and the process by which you will attain it. The plan encourages you to organize tasks into functions, and then helps people grasp the logic of each of those functions. This in turn permits you to bring new employees up to speed quickly.

There are numerous books and seminars on the subject of practice management, but they focus on making you a better accountant. I want to teach you something else that you've never been taught before: how to be a manager. It has nothing to do with conventional practice management and everything to do with thinking like an entrepreneur.

The Planning Triangle

As we discussed in the Introduction, every accounting practice is a company, every accounting business is a company, and every accounting enterprise is a company. Yet the differences between the three are extraordinary. Although all three may offer accounting services, *how* they do what they do is completely different.

The trouble with most companies owned by accountants is that they are dependent on the accountant. That's because they're a practice—the smallest, most limited form a company can take. Practices are formed around the technician, whether an accountant or a roofer.

You may choose in the beginning to form a practice, but you should understand its limitations. The company called a *practice* depends on the owner—that is, the accountant. The company called a *business* depends on other people plus a system by which that business does what it does. Once your practice becomes a business, you can replicate it, turning it into an *enterprise*.

Consider the example of Martland Accounting Offices. The clients don't come in asking for Douglas Martland, although he is one of the top CPAs around. After all, he can handle only so many cases a day and be in only one location at a time

Yet Douglas wants to offer his high-quality services to more people in the community. If he has reliable systems in place—systems that any qualified associate accountant can learn to use—he has created a business and it can be replicated. Douglas can then go on to offer his services—which demand his guidance, not his presence—in a multitude of different settings. He can open dozens of accounting practices, none of which needs Douglas Martland himself, except in the role of entrepreneur.

Is your accounting company going to be a practice, a business, or an enterprise? Planning is crucial to answering this all-important question. Whatever you choose to do must be communicated by your plan, which is really three interrelated plans in one. We call it the Planning Triangle, and it consists of the following:

- Business plan
- Practice plan
- Completion plan

The three plans form a triangle, with the business plan at the base, the practice plan in the center, and the completion plan at the apex.

The business plan determines *who* you are (the business), the practice plan determines *what* you do (the specific focus of your accounting practice), and the completion plan determines *how* you do it (the fulfillment process).

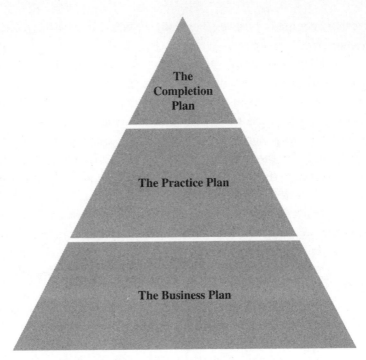

FIGURE 5.1   The Planning Triangle.

By looking at the planning triangle, we see that the three critical plans are interconnected. The connections among them are established by asking the following questions:

1. Who are we?
2. What do we do?
3. How do we do it?

Who are we? is purely a strategic question.
What do we do? is both a strategic and a tactical question.
How do we do it? is both a strategic and a tactical question.
Strategic questions shape the vision and destiny of your business, of which your practice is only one essential component.

Tactical questions turn that vision into reality. Thus, strategic questions provide the foundation for tactical questions, just as the base provides the foundation for the middle and the apex of your planning triangle.

First ask: What do we do and how do we do it . . . *strategically?*

And then ask: What do we do and how do we do it . . . *practically?*

Let's look at how the three plans will help you develop your practice.

The Business Plan

Your business plan will determine what you choose to do in your accounting practice and the way you choose to do it. Without a business plan, your practice can do little more than survive. And even that will take more than a little luck.

Without a business plan, you're treading water in a deep pool with no shore in sight. You're working against the natural flow.

I'm not talking about the traditional business plan taught in business schools. No, this business plan reads like a story—the most important story you will ever tell.

Your business plan must clearly describe the following:

- The business you are creating
- The purpose it will serve
- The vision it will pursue
- The process through which you will turn that vision into reality
- The way money will be used to realize your vision

Build your business plan with *business* language, not *practice* language (the language of the accountant). Make sure the plan focuses on matters of interest to your lenders and shareholders rather than just your technicians. It should rely on demographics and psychographics to tell you who buys and why; it should also include projections for return on investment and return on equity. Use it to detail both the market and the strategy through which you intend to become a leader in that market, not as an accountant but as a business enterprise.

The business plan, though absolutely essential, is only one of three critical plans every accountant needs to create and implement. Now let's take a look at the practice plan.

The Practice Plan

The practice plan includes everything an accountant needs to know, have, and do in order to deliver his or her promise to a client on time, every time.

Every task should prompt you to ask three questions:

1. What do I need to know?
2. What do I need to have?
3. What do I need to do?

What Do I Need to *Know?*

What information do I need to satisfy my promise on time, every time, exactly as promised? In order to recognize what you need to know, you must understand the expectations of others, including your clients, your associates, and other employees. Are you clear on those expectations? Don't make the mistake of assuming you know. Instead, create a Need-to-Know Checklist to make sure you ask all the necessary questions.

A Need-to-Know Checklist might look like this:

- What are the expectations of my clients?
- What are the expectations of my administrators?
- What are the expectations of my associate accountants?
- What are the expectations of my staff?

What Do I Need to *Have?*

This question raises the issue of resources—namely, money, people, and time. If you don't have enough money to finance operations, how can you fulfill those expectations without creating cash-flow problems? If you don't have enough trained people, what happens then? And if you don't have enough time to manage your practice, what happens when you can't be in two places at once?

Don't assume that you can get what you need when you need it. Most often, you can't. And even if you can get what you need at the last minucte, you'll pay dearly for it.

What Do I Need to *Do?*

The focus here is on actions to be started and finished. What do I need to do to fulfill the expectations of this client on time, every time, exactly as promised? For example, what exactly are the steps to perform when seeing someone with an IRS lien or a failure to file federal and state taxes for a four-year period?

Your clients fall into distinct categories, and those categories make up your practice. The best accounting practices will invariably focus on fewer and fewer categories as they discover the importance of doing one thing better than anyone else.

Answering the question *What do I need to do?* demands a series of action plans, including:

- The objective to be achieved
- The standards by which you will know that the objective has been achieved
- The benchmarks you need to reach in order for the objective to be achieved
- The function/person accountable for the completion of the benchmarks
- The budget for the completion of each benchmark
- The time by which each benchmark must be completed

Your action plans should become the foundation for your completion plans. And the reason you need completion plans is to ensure that everything you do not only is realistic but can also be managed.

The Completion Plan

If the practice plan gives you results and provides you with standards, the completion plan tells you everything you need to know about every benchmark in the practice plan—that is, how you're going to fulfill client expectations on time, every time, as promised. In other words, how you are going to perform your initial customer assessment, how you are going to communicate your recommendations, how you are going to educate a customer about the changed processes you are recommending.

The completion plan is essentially the operations manual, providing information about the details of doing tactical work. It is a guide that tells the people responsible for doing that work exactly how to do it.

Every completion plan becomes a part of the knowledge base of your business. No completion plan goes to waste. Every completion plan becomes a kind of textbook that explains to new employees or new associates joining your team how your practice operates in a way that distinguishes it from all other accounting practices.

To return to an earlier example, the completion plan for making a Big Mac is explicitly described in the *McDonald's Operation Manual,* as is every completion plan needed to run a McDonald's business.

The completion plan for an accountant might include the step-by-step details of how to analyze the internal accounting controls, workflow efficiency, or current technology platform of clients—in contrast to how everyone else has learned to do it. Of course, anyone who works in accounting has learned about these subjects. They've learned to do it the same way everyone else has learned to do it. But if you are going to stand out as unique in the minds of your clients, employees, and others, you must invent your own ways of doing even ordinary things.

Perhaps you'll decide that, as a mandatory part of your client-assessment procedure, you feature a client portal on your web site; when clients log in, they can enter answers to your assessment questionnaire and then view an interactive progression of suggested steps and conclusions. If no other accountant has ever taken the time to explain the benefits and steps of a platform or procedure change to the client, you'll immediately set yourself apart. You must constantly raise the questions: *How do we do it here? How* should *we do it here?*

The quality of your answers will determine how effectively you distinguish your practice from every other accountant's practice.

Benchmarks

You can measure the movement of your practice—from what it is today to what it will be in the future—using business *benchmarks*.

These are the goals you want your business to achieve during its lifetime.

Your benchmarks should include the following:

- Financial benchmarks
- Emotional benchmarks (the impact your practice will have on everyone who comes into contact with it)
- Performance benchmarks
- Client benchmarks (Who are your clients? Why do they come to you? What will your practice give them that no one else will?)
- Employee benchmarks (How do you grow people? How do you find people who want to grow? How do you create a school in your practice that will teach your people skills they can't learn anywhere else?)

Your business benchmarks will reflect (1) the position your practice will hold in the minds and hearts of your clients, employees, and investors and (2) how you intend to make that position a reality through the systems you develop.

Your benchmarks describe how your management team will take shape and what systems you will need to develop so that your managers, just like McDonald's managers, can produce the results for which they will be held accountable.

Benefits of the Planning Triangle

By implementing the planning triangle, you will discover these things:

- What your practice will look, act, and feel like when it's fully evolved

- When that's going to happen
- How much money you will make

And much, much more.

These, then, are the primary purposes of the three critical plans:

1. To clarify precisely what needs to be done to get what the accountant wants from his or her practice and life
2. To define the specific steps by which it will happen

First *this* must happen, then *that* must happen. One, two, three. By monitoring your progress, step by step, you can determine whether you're on the right track.

That's what planning is all about. It's about creating a standard—a yardstick—against which you will be able to measure your performance.

Failing to create such a standard is like throwing a piece of straw into a hurricane. Who knows where that straw will land?

Have you taken the leap? Have you accepted that the word *business* and the word *practice* are not synonymous? That a practice relies on the accountant and a business relies on other people plus a system?

Because many accountants are control freaks, 99 percent of today's accounting firms are practices, not businesses.

The result, as a friend of mine says, is that "Accountants are spending all day stamping out fires when all around them the forest is ablaze. They're out of touch, and they'd better take control of the practice before someone else does."

Because accountants are never taught to think like business-people, the auditor is forever at war with the businessperson. This is especially evident in large, multidiscipline practices, where accountants lacking the knowledge of how to run a business try to control accountants. They usually end up treating each other as combatants. In fact, the single greatest reason accountants become entrepreneurs is to divorce themselves from such bureaucratically-minded colleagues and to begin to reinvent the accounting enterprise.

That's you. Now the divorce is over and a new love affair has begun. You're an accountant with a plan! Who wouldn't want to do business with such a person?

Now let's take the next step in our strategic odyssey. Let's take a closer look at the subject of *management*. But, before we do, let's listen to what Darren has to say about *planning*.

CHAPTER 6

The Value of Taking Aim

M. Darren Root

Plan your work for today and every day, then work your plan.
—Norman Vincent Peale

Henry David Thoreau wrote, "In the long run, men hit only what they aim at." I believe this quote expresses Michael's core message in Chapter 5. It's all about envisioning the end and developing the plan to get there (*what we aim at*).

The previous chapter offers a clear road map for transitioning your practice into a business. And to do this, you must plan. Unfortunately, accountants often overlook the basic message of creating a plan because of the chaotic nature of running a firm. When you are constantly mired in work, who has time to plan? This is a common way of thinking in the accounting profession, and it needs to change.

Michael's planning message is one I've implemented in my practice with great success. In fact, it has worked so well that I created a guide for the accounting profession based on the tenets Michael advocates. His message is also a cornerstone of my Next Generation Accounting Firm™ presentation, which I offer across the country and to firms that I coach.

Like you, I know all too well about harsh deadlines—our profession is designed around them. We have the traditional busy season, quarterly payroll tax deadlines, W-2s, 1099s, monthly financial statements . . . and the list goes on. As a result, most accountants have only learned to juggle deadlines and deliver product—not how to build a streamlined, automated system to support their business.

To help build such a system, I have developed a framework, comprehensive workbook, and model to ease accountants through the planning process. Before you can review and apply these elements, however, it's important to complete a thorough evaluation of your practice.

In my experience, accountants are the worst at conducting an honest analysis of their own firms. This is not to say that the profession is against honest evaluation; rather, the problem arises from a busy schedule. When mired in the tedious tasks that define tax season, for example, who has time for a comprehensive analysis? But busy or not, if accountants want to change how they do business and transition from technician to leader, they must make the time.

So, on to the first question: What should you evaluate? The answer: everything.

The key to a good evaluation is understanding where your firm stands today. What services do you offer, and are you focusing on the services you perform best and that drive your economic engine? Who are your clients? Do you deal with a wide range, or have you narrowed down your client base to only those you desire—that is, to those who fit your defined services?

First, let's talk about the services you offer and why. When you started your firm, you probably took the same path as the rest of us—you took on anyone who walked through the door. As a result, your services were formed based on the clients' needs. Over the years, most accountants never stray from this model, which means they still offer an array of services instead of a well defined few.

Offering too many services is one of the biggest barriers to creating a business. Accounting professionals are so busy keeping up with disparate tasks associated with a variety of services that they simply don't have time to plan or implement change. This keeps the accountant at the technician level. By defining a select few services your firm can perform efficiently and within a streamlined workflow, you are better positioned to produce more work with less effort. I say it time and time again in my presentation: Define your areas of "greatness," and focus on those areas to drive revenue.

This leads me to the topic of clients. Successful accounting firms are in a position to select their clients. If the client doesn't fit the service model, that client doesn't go any further than a prospect. It's a simple connection. If you've defined your services, you can define your client base. For example, in my practice, we provide Back Office Support System (BOSS™), accounting, tax, and payroll services. We do not take on clients that fall outside of this service model (such as audits, reviews, nonprofits, and trusts). We also focus on service-based businesses such as physicians, dentists, attorneys, and architects. By focusing on a defined client base, we excel at the services we offer and continue to build the business based on this desired clientele.

Let's take a quick look at how most firms operate today to gain a better understanding of the issues that face the profession.

For most of you, your current clients have been with you from the beginning and run the gamut in regard to the services they require. Most likely this means you don't have uniform processes for how work is performed and completed. In other words, the client, not the firm, defines the process. Throw in the facts that your clients use their own internal accounting systems and have their own processes in place, and what you have is a mess. Combined, all this puts the accountant in reactive mode, having to complete work based on the specifics of each client account. In the end, your clients are setting the pace and calling the shots— not you. What a nightmare!

And then there's technology. Like services and client base, technology presents its own issues if not applied wisely.

Technologies for the accounting profession have advanced rapidly, offering a slew of powerful systems that can help accountants streamline processes firmwide. For example, the Software as a Service (SaaS) model enables firms to go completely paperless and work in the Cloud. Integrated software solutions are also available, allowing data to flow seamlessly from write-up, to tax, to practice management applications—eliminating the need to reenter data from app to app.

Although the technology is readily available, creating the ideal system requires firms to take time to research what is available and evaluate how solutions work together. Technology is the key to proper delivery of services to clients, not to mention the means by which your staff can work efficiently and with ease. I still remember the days of working on weekends just to keep up with e-mails and voice mails that went ignored during the week when I was buried in client work. Because technology is at the core of an efficient system, it must also be part of a firm's initial evaluation. What does your technology look like?

That's a lot to think about, but it drives home my point. If you don't take the time to plan, your firm will continue to exist in chaos and you will remain in reactive mode. Taking the time to evaluate your practice critically is an investment you can't afford not to make.

Let's not kid ourselves: There will always be tax returns to process, financial statements to compile, and calls and e-mails to answer. However, with proper planning you will find you have the time to complete these tasks during a normal workday because your business is operating at peak efficiency. Reading the words and understanding the concepts are not enough; you must take action to see the true rewards.

Let's begin where Michael did. First, we'll discus your business plan, then your practice plan, and finally your completion plan.

Your Business Plan

The big question: What business do you want to be in?

It's a simple question, and one that must be answered before you can begin moving forward with change. A broad definition of your ideal practice is at the heart of your business plan, providing a clear picture of what must be accomplished. It allows you to create a mental picture of what will get you to your desired result.

To define "who you are," that is, what business do you want to be in, you have to ask yourself other questions. What are your strengths or core competencies (your areas of "greatness")? What services do you want to perform each day? What are you passionate about? What are you currently doing, and where do you want to go from there? As you ask yourself these questions, be sure to write down your answers, create lists, and continually work to refine your definition of "what business you want to be in." Once you have a clear, concise statement on paper, you've taken the first big step toward developing a sound business plan.

I found that creating my business plan required a lot of soul searching and tough decision making. For example, narrowing my client list to include those within defined niches, instead of taking on every client that walked through the door. Or hiring more staff to take over the work for which I had always maintained control. Working through those tough decisions, though, brings clarity to your plan and allows you to move forward rapidly.

As you continue to develop your business plan, it's also important to remember that your business is personal. It's personal to you, as well as to your family, employees, vendors, and clients. So treat it as such. Allot the time required to develop a plan that will be pleasing to everyone involved—since everyone around you will be affected by the change.

Also, be aware that your plan is organic—always changing and growing. Your business plan should be treated as a living document to be reviewed and enhanced as your business grows. Just as you have evolved over the years, so will your business and the plan that supports it.

Let's start the process. Have your computer or a pencil and paper ready.

Begin your business plan with an accurate account of where you stand—a balance sheet of sorts. Start by making a comprehensive list of the services you currently provide. Include in your list all the industries you service (for example, construction, manufacturing, restaurants, and so on). Putting this information on paper allows you to see just how all-over-the-board you may be and will get you thinking about how you can better define service options. Of the firms I've coached, the majority conclude that they are trying to be all things to all clients, which is a deterrent to true mastery of any given service or niche. That said, at the heart of your plan is a clear vision of the business you are in and what markets you serve.

Also spend some time thinking about your strengths and your firm's strengths. Because you are the architect of your future, focus on the services you actually like to perform. Imagine that your firm focused on a limited number of service offerings—services for which you and your staff exhibit exceptional levels of competency: What would your typical day look like? As firm owner who has defined my services, I can tell you that my days run smoothly and my staff is happy.

To be successful, you need to develop a burning desire to go to work each day. You can develop this by creating a work environment built on services you have a passion to perform, as well as clients that you enjoy serving. So, ask yourself: What services do I want to offer? Will these services create a work environment that gets me out of bed, excited, and ready to head out to the office? Passion drives happiness, and this feeling is contagious. A positive work culture is felt and perpetuated by your staff, family, and clients. You can obtain this type of culture if you have the right business plan in place.

For the most part, the broad accounting profession has not adopted the message of defining services and client base. Change is hard and scary; I understand this as well as anyone. However, accountants must specialize if they expect to transform their firms into businesses. Just look at other professions. Doctors who specialize become experts in their chosen fields, making them highly sought after and in a position to charge more for services. The same is true for attorneys, creative firms, and technology vendors. By specializing in a defined area, these businesses are not compelled to take on just any client who walks through the door.

Once you define the scope of your practice, your business becomes more manageable because there is less to, well, manage. Processes become standardized, workflows streamlined, and clients easily categorized because your business model is clear and concise. Can you imagine anyone walking into Starbucks and asking for a burger? That doesn't happen because Starbucks has a well-defined business model, which dictates their clientele and service expectations.

During my college years at Indiana University one of my professors said, "The key to success is figuring out what you're really good at and having the clear conviction to stay focused enough and not veer off course." Little did I know then the impact this advice would have as I built my firm. This is the same advice Michael and I offer in this book. I hope it has the same impact on transforming your practice.

Your Practice Plan

The big question: What services and niches define your business?

In the previous section, on business plans, we discussed the idea of defining who you are—who you want to be and the type of business you want to operate. Your business plan identifies your core competencies and strengths—offering a solid base upon which you can begin to mold your business.

With a clear picture of your mission in place, your practice plan will take you to the next level. In this plan, you get down to the details and select the exact services you will offer and the niche industries you will serve.

Your practice plan, if developed accurately, will help you identify what you do more clearly. These are the questions you will answer at this phase of the process:

- What specific services, niches, and clients will you serve?
- And more important, which will you eliminate?
- What geographic areas will you serve?
- How much do you want to grow your business?

In creating your business plan, you created a list of all the services you currently provide, as well as the industries you support. Then you used this list to identify your areas of strength—that is, the services and industries that support your core competencies. In essence, you took an inventory of where you are today. Now, use this comprehensive list to identify a defined set of services and industries going forward . . . and abandon the rest.

This is a hard step to take, especially if you've provided an array of services to a variety of clients for many years. However, unless you whittle down your practice to something manageable, change is highly unlikely. You must keep in mind that you can standardize the way you work only if you also standardize your offerings.

Your service model will inevitably drive your client base. So once you've identified your core services and the niche industries that best fit your model, you should conduct a thorough review of your existing client list. Determine which clients fit your model—your "A" clients. In my firm, our "A" demographic includes those clients who require our core services (bookkeeping, accounting, payroll, and corporate and individual tax) and who fit our defined industry targets (service-based businesses such as physicians, attorneys, and architects). By creating a client base that fits your service model, you are better equipped to lead clients down a successful path based on your focused niche expertise.

Next, identify defined geographic areas for your niche clients. By focusing on defined areas, you can better target potential clients. It's much easier to find the niche clients you desire within a defined area. Using the Web, telephone book, or other marketing media, identify foundations, events, and organizations that provide the proper venues to capture prospects.

As I mentioned in Chapter 4, the accounting profession is designed to produce recurring revenue. Based on the decisions you make regarding your services, clients, niches, and geographic service areas, you can build strong, consistent revenue streams that require far less time to manage than you spend on them now. Just consider the advantages of a uniform, streamlined structure:

- Enables you to select your desired client base
- Supports uniform processes for each service you offer—which means every staff member processes work the same way
- Allows you, not the client, to control workflow
- Significantly increases efficiency firmwide, so you can take on more work with fewer resources
- Supports a structured marketing program by allowing you to create targeted programs for defined niches
- Offers you and your staff true life–work balance
- Enables you to transition from working *in* your firm to working *on* your firm—moving from technician to savvy business leader

With the right practice plan in place, you can realize all of these benefits. Remember, it's about taking aim and then plotting your course to get there.

Your Completion Plan

The big question: Now that you've defined your business, how will you deliver?

Your completion plan helps you identify the systems and processes required to deliver the model you've defined. This is where the rubber meets the road. Defining who you are is all well and good, but it's of little worth if you cannot deliver.

The key to every successful business is the systems and processes in place. Take McDonald's as an example. Each franchise operates the same way—from the ordering process to the system for food preparation. The same is true for Starbucks. No matter the location or the individual employees, the process is the same. McDonald's and Starbucks have precise systems in place to ensure uniform processes and efficiency of workflow.

When I use these examples while coaching firms, often I get the same response: "I run an accounting firm—every client is different. This is not retail, so I can't possibly do what McDonald's and Starbucks have done." But it's not about retail versus an accounting firm. It's about the *system*. With the right system in place, any business can operate in a uniform, efficient manner.

Bottom line: If you want to operate your practice as a business, this step is crucial. It is where you will transform a chaotic and inefficient practice, which relies on you as a technician, into a business that functions like a well-oiled, well-maintained machine—whether or not you are there. And that's what you want—the ability to take yourself out of your firm without a major breakdown in workflow.

Go back to your defined core services. Your completion plan should include a detailed strategy for how you will deliver each service. For example, to support a standardized tax workflow, you must define a process that includes how client data is collected, processed, and delivered. For a 1040 tax return, this process might include these steps:

1. Collect initial client data via an online organizer within the client's portal.
2. Organize client data and source documents within a single PDF using a SaaS-based scan-and-organize application.
3. Seamlessly flow data from the PDF into the application using integrated tax software, eliminating manual data entry.
4. Allow online review of the tax return through the client's portal.

5. E-file tax return through tax software.
6. Deliver completed return to the client online within their portal.
7. Invoice client online within their portal.
8. Accept client's payment online.

You must document all processes to ensure that everyone is applying the same steps for each service offered. This provides a checklist of tasks for staff and clients and a well-designed document for educating new staff. Remember, you are the architect of your firm, so it is within your power to lead staff and clients where you want them to go. Doing so eliminates the chaos that occurs when clients dictate the process and multiple staff members apply disparate procedures to deliver the same service.

Your completion plan is the main document that allows you and your staff to execute services efficiently and effortlessly. It keeps everyone on the same page at all times. The processes defined within your completion plan support a broad, standardized system. And the *order* that a sound plan brings about is invaluable!

CHAPTER 7

On the Subject of Management

Michael E. Gerber

Good management consists of showing average people how to do the
work of superior people.

—John D. Rockefeller

E very accountant, including Steve, eventually faces the
issues of management. Most face it badly.

Why do so many accountants suffer from a kind of
paralysis when it comes to dealing with management? Why are so
few able to get their accounting practice to work the way they
want it to and to run it on time? Why are their managers (if they
have any) seemingly so inept?

There are two main problems. First, the accountant usually abdicates responsibility for management by hiring an office manager. Thus, the accountant is working hand and glove with someone who is supposed to do the managing. But the accountant is unmanageable himself!

The accountant doesn't think like a manager because he doesn't think he *is* a manager. He's an accountant! He rules the roost. And so he gets the office manager to take care of stuff like scheduling appointments, keeping his calendar, collecting receivables, hiring and firing, and much more.

Second, no matter who does the managing, that person usually has a completely dysfunctional idea of what it means to manage. He is trying to manage people, contrary to what is needed.

We often hear that a good manager must be a "people person." Someone who loves to nourish, figure out, support, care for, teach, baby, monitor, mentor, direct, track, motivate, and—if all else fails—threaten or beat up her people.

Don't believe it. Management has far less to do with people than you've been led to think.

In fact, despite the claims of every management book written by management gurus (who have seldom managed anything), no one—with the exception of a few bloodthirsty tyrants—has ever learned how to manage people.

And the reason is simple: *People are almost impossible to manage.*

Yes, it's true. People are unmanageable. They're inconsistent, unpredictable, unchangeable, unrepentant, irrepressible, and generally impossible.

Doesn't knowing this make you feel better? Now you understand why you've had all those problems! Do you feel the relief, the heavy stone lifted from your chest?

The time has come to understand fully what management is really all about. Rather than managing *people*, management is really all about managing a *process*, a step-by-step way of doing things, which, combined with other processes, becomes a system. Here are some examples:

- The process for on-time scheduling
- The process for answering the telephone
- The process for greeting a customer
- The process for organizing customer files

Thus, a process is the step-by-step way of doing something over time. Considered as a whole, these processes are a system:

- The on-time scheduling system
- The telephone answering system
- The client greeting system
- The file organization system

Instead of managing people, then, the truly effective manager has been taught a system for managing a process through which people get things done.

More precisely, managers and their people, *together*, manage the processes—the systems—that comprise your business. Management is less about *who* gets things done in your business than about *how* things get done.

In fact, great managers are not fascinated with people, but with how things get done through people. Great managers are masters at figuring out how to get things done effectively and efficiently through people using extraordinary systems.

Great managers constantly ask key questions:

- What is the result we intend to produce?
- Are we producing that result every single time?

- If we're not producing that result every single time, why not?
- If we are producing that result every single time, how could we produce even better results?
- Do we lack a system? If so, what would that system look like if we were to create it?
- If we have a system, why aren't we using it?

And so forth.

In short, a great manager can leave the office fully assured that it will run at least as well as it does when he is physically in the room.

Great managers are those who use a great management system. A system that shouts, "This is *how* we manage here." Not, "This is *who* manages here."

In a truly effective company, how you manage is always more important than who manages. Provided a system is in place, how you manage is transferable, whereas who manages isn't. *How* you manage can be taught, whereas *who* manages can't be.

When a company is dependent on *who* manages—Katie, Kim, or Kevin—that business is in serious jeopardy. Because when Katie, Kim, or Kevin leaves, that business has to start over again. What an enormous waste of time and resources!

Even worse, when a company is dependent on *who* manages, you can bet all the managers in that business are doing their own thing. What could be more unproductive than 10 managers, each of whom manages in a unique way? How in the world could you possibly manage those managers?

The answer is: You can't. Because it takes you right back to trying to manage *people* again.

And, as I hope you now know, that's impossible.

In this chapter, I often refer to managers in the plural. I know that most accountants have only one manager—the office manager. And so you may be thinking that a management system isn't so important in a small accounting practice. After all, the office manager does whatever an office manager does (and thank God because you don't want to do it).

But if your practice is ever going to turn into the business it could become, and if that business is ever going to turn into the enterprise of your dreams, then the questions you ask about how the office manager manages your affairs are critical ones. Because until you come to grips with your dual role as owner and key employee, and with the relationship your manager has to those two roles, your practice/business/enterprise will never realize its potential, thus the need for a management system.

Management System

What, then, is a management system?

The E-Myth says that a management system is the method by which every manager innovates, quantifies, orchestrates, and then monitors the systems through which your practice produces the results you expect.

According to the E-Myth, a manager's job is simple:

A manager's job is to invent the systems through which the owner's vision is consistently and faithfully manifested at the operating level of the business.

Which brings us right back to the purpose of your business and the need for an entrepreneurial vision.

Are you beginning to see what I'm trying to share with you? That your business is one single thing? And that all the subjects we're discussing here—money, planning, management, and so on—are all about doing one thing well?

That one thing is the one thing your practice is intended to do: distinguish your accounting business from all others.

It is the manager's role to make certain it all fits. And it's your role as entrepreneur to make sure your manager knows what the business is supposed to look, act, and feel like when it's finally done. As clearly as you know how, you must convey to your manager what you know to be true—your vision, your picture of the business when it's finally done. In this way, your vision is translated into your manager's marching orders every day he or she reports to work.

Unless that vision is embraced by your manager, you and your people will suffer from the tyranny of routine. And your business will suffer from it, too.

Now let's move on to *people*. Because, as we know, it's people who are causing all our problems. But before we do, let's hear what Darren has to say about *management*.

CHAPTER 8

Management by Design

M. Darren Root

Management is no longer developing work through people. Real management is developing people through work.

—Anonymous

I n Chapter 6, I introduced the necessity of implementing efficient processes and establishing a system to support efficient delivery of services. The same is true for managing people. When you have standardized processes in place for all the services your firm performs, you simplify training and shorten the learning curve for staff. Essentially, you make your employees' jobs easier. And when things are easy, staff is happy—and you spend less time dealing with complaints and problems.

A well-run office also tends to attract highly qualified job candidates, providing you with a better pool of prospects. In the end, a systemized business is better equipped to retain and attract good people and to repel those who are not a good fit.

I'm sure everyone has experienced dealing with a "bad" employee. As managers, we've all wondered what makes some employees outstanding while others fail miserably. Historically, managers have thought that the bad apples were simply bad hires or not self-starters. And although this may be true occasionally, more often than not, many less-than-outstanding employees fall victim to organizational flaws—specifically a lack of order.

Over the years, I've had my share of inadequate hires. I would bring on a new employee, expecting the highest level of work and professionalism. Not an unrealistic expectation, right? My recruiting philosophy was that if I hired a person with the right experience and skills, they would easily meld into the culture and perform well. If the hire did not work out, I would just write it off as "not a good fit."

Of course, I have also hired many outstanding employees. However, in the absence of a structured system, simply hiring outstanding employees was not without its issues. Those employees who performed well had the required experience and an innate ability to create unique processes to support their duties. Initially, I viewed this as a good characteristic. In reality, what I had was a cadre of high performers who had all installed their own custom system around their respective positions. Although the work was getting done, each system was unique to its creator—so each employee represented the sole source of knowledge for a given position in the firm. I also found that most of the systems created did not match the broad vision I had for the firm. I was left with disparate processes and a culture of managing individual employees and their individual processes.

This cycle went on for years until I read *The E-Myth*. I zoomed in on what Michael said about people: "They are unmanageable, they're inconsistent, unpredictable, unchangeable, unrepentant, irrepressible, and generally impossible." Even worse, I realized that these *unmanageable* people were being managed by a "lunatic"— me. Understanding that people are innately unchangeable and that I was practicing under the title of lunatic, not leader, I knew I needed to make some changes, quickly.

Michael made me realize that I needed to stop trying to manage employees and invest time in developing processes and procedures. Once I had standard processes in place, the process, not the people, would dictate the work. This would correct two major issues:

1. Employees would no longer be responsible for creating their own systems.
2. I would no longer be responsible for managing individual staff members.

Let's look at each of these issues in more detail.

Relieving employees of having to create their own systems opens the door for firmwide uniform processes. Creating a single process for each service or duty within the office means everyone is performing a task the same way. A uniform process is far more efficient than having individual staff members dictate how a task is performed, and it eliminates the problems that arise when only one person possesses the knowledge to perform any duty. Staff will also feel a sense of relief, thanks to the order that standardizing processes offers. A chaotic environment doesn't breed happy employees.

Eliminating the need to manage individuals and individual systems freed a great deal of my time—time I could contribute to tweaking and enhancing our broad system. It also allowed me to transition from a technician, always caught up in task-oriented issues, to a true leader in my firm. Best of all, I was able to leave the title of lunatic behind, which greatly benefited my staff and myself.

From this epiphany, I set out to create standard processes for everything we did in our office, documenting each and training staff accordingly. The outcome was phenomenal. Staff turnover plummeted; no one was leaving the firm. Efficiency increased many times over, and our realization more than doubled in the first year.

Providing a uniform system created a sense of ease among the staff. Employees, no longer burdened with creating and maintaining their own processes, felt a sense of freedom because they were no longer solely responsible for a single duty. It also opened the door for cross-training, which my employees love.

Personally, I found hiring new staff to be much easier. No longer did I have to focus only on experience and skills. With process as king, I knew that, for the most part, staff could be developed through the work. That meant that I was also able to hire based on personality and potential fit within the culture. By basing hiring on all these elements, I was able to find excellent staff who could both handle the work and quickly acclimate to the firm's working environment.

A quick note on realization: In our profession, many factors associated with realization exist, such as fixed-fee billing versus traditional hourly billing, effective implementation of technology, and procuring the right clients. In my opinion, however, the major factor that drives increase in realization is the existence of proper systems and processes.

Through established systems, staff can come to work each day and know what is expected. They also benefit from having the proper tools and resources to accomplish tasks with ease and efficiency. A study by the American Accounting Association, "Healthy Lifestyle as a Coping Mechanism for Role Stress in Public Accounting" (Jones, Norman, & Weir 2010), reported that the three main contributors to job burnout are role ambiguity, role conflict, and role overload. Putting standard processes in place alleviates ambiguity of roles and conflict caused from overlapping tasks.

Michael claims that, innately, people don't want to be managed, so why should we try? Leadership is where we can best spend our time. When you create a reliable, proven system, people can manage themselves and their own workloads, while you are left to lead the organization to bigger and better places. Leading people, not managing them, also leaves room for your staff to grow and reach their potential.

Setting the Course

Implementing the right systems allows you and your employees to see your business in a whole new way. As stated earlier in the book, with the right changes, we put ourselves in the position to expertly lead clients in the right financial direction. I think this is also true for staff. We should be creating a business that leads staff in the direction they should go . . . plotting their course for success in our firms. This means giving them an organized, simplified structure in which to work, as well as the tools required to accomplish their work. What you don't want to do is allow staff to create their own processes and set the course for your firm.

In your broad plan, you should create the course that puts you in the lead position and provides you with the confidence to instruct your staff on how things operate and how tasks will be completed. How do you do this? By creating a format for every "input" into your firm—whether it's a phone call, a tax return, or a new client intake. There is a process for every task. Identify each task's process and document it.

Imagine for a moment that you have designed and implemented a structured process for a 1040 tax return—from initial client contact to completion of the return. You've documented each step is documented and put in place the necessary technologies to support a completely electronic process. Not only is everyone following the same process and promoting maximum efficiency, but you've also improved your ability to track and monitor projects. At any point, you can pinpoint the project's status—no matter who the client is or which staff member is handling it—because the process is always the same!

Now imagine that you have a structured process for every task or service in your firm. Everyone is answering the phone the same way, new clients are handled in a uniform manner, and every tax or accounting project flows through your firm seamlessly. Your firm is no longer just a firm, but a well-oiled economic machine. What staff member wouldn't enjoy working in such an environment?

On the Subject of People

Michael E. Gerber

Very few people go to the doctor when they have a cold. They go to the theatre instead.

—Oscar Wilde

Every accountant I've ever met has complained about people.

About employees: "They come in late, they go home early, they have the focus of an antique camera!"

About the IRS: "They're just out to get my clients, and they're inconsistent, willful, and bullying!"

About clients: "They dump the equivalent of two shoeboxes full of receipts on my desk and expect me to have their returns done yesterday!"

People, people, people. Every accountant's nemesis. And at the heart of it all are the people who work for you.

"By the time I tell them how to do it, I could have done it 20 times myself!" "How come nobody listens to what I say?" "Why is it nobody ever does what I ask them to do?" Does this sound like you?

So what's the problem with people? To answer that, think back to the last time you walked into an accountant's office. What did you see in the people's faces?

Most people working in accounting are harried. You can see it in their expressions. They're negative. They're bad-spirited. They're humorless. And with good reason. After all, they're surrounded by people who have tax problems or who are suffering cash flow problems, or—worst case scenario—may even be a candidate for a business closure. And many are either terrified or depressed. They don't want to be there.

Is it any wonder employees at most accounting practices are disgruntled? They're surrounded by unhappy people all day. They're answering the same questions 24/7. And most of the time, the accountant has no time for them. He or she is too busy leading a dysfunctional life.

Working with people brings great joy—and monumental frustration. And so it is with accountants and their people. But why? And what can we do about it?

Let's look at the typical accountant—who this person is and isn't.

Most accountants are unprepared to use other people to get results. Not because they can't find people, but because they are fixated on getting the results themselves. In other words, most accountants are not the businesspeople they need to be; *they're technicians suffering from an entrepreneurial seizure.*

Am I talking about you? What were you doing before you became an entrepreneur?

Were you an associate accountant working for a Big Four firm? A large regional organization? A mid-size practice? A small practice?

Didn't you imagine owning your own practice as the way out?

Didn't you think that because you knew how to do the technical work—because you knew so much about tax strategies, financial planning, and internal controls—you were automatically prepared to create a practice that does that type of work?

Didn't you figure that by creating your own practice you could dump the boss once and for all? How else to get rid of that impossible person, the one driving you crazy, the one who never let you do your own thing, the one who was the main reason you decided to take the leap into a business of your own in the first place?

Didn't you start your own practice so that you could become your own boss?

And didn't you imagine that once you became your own boss, you would be free to do whatever you wanted to do—and to take home *all* the money?

Honestly, isn't that what you imagined? So you went into business for yourself and immediately dove into work.

Doing it, doing it, doing it.

Busy, busy, busy.

Until one day you realized (or maybe not) that you were doing all of the work. You were doing everything you knew how to do, plus a lot more you knew nothing about. Building sweat equity, you thought.

In reality, a technician suffering from an entrepreneurial seizure.

You were just hoping to make a buck in your own practice. And sometimes you did earn a wage. But other times you didn't. You were the one signing the checks all right, but they went to other people.

Does this sound familiar? Is it driving you crazy?

Well, relax, because we're going to show you the right way to do it this time.

Read carefully. Be mindful of the moment. You are about to learn the secret you've been waiting for all your working life.

The People Law

It's critical to know this about the working life of accountants who own their own accounting practice: *Without people, you don't own a practice; you own a job.* And it can be the worst job in the world because you're working for a lunatic! (Nothing personal—but we've got to face facts.)

Let me state what every accountant knows: Without people, you're going to have to do it all yourself. Without human help, you're doomed to try to do too much. This isn't a breakthrough idea, but it's amazing how many accountants ignore the truth. They end up knocking themselves out, 10 to 12 hours a day. They try to do more, but less actually gets done.

The load can double you over and leave you panting. In addition to the work you're used to doing, you may also have to do the books . . . and the organizing . . . and the filing. You'll have to do the planning and the scheduling. When you own your own practice, dealing with the endless flow of minor details is never-ending, as I'm sure you've found out. Like painting the Golden Gate Bridge, it's endless. Which puts it beyond the realm of human possibility. Until you discover how to get it done by somebody else, it will continue on and on until you're a burned-out husk.

But with others helping you, things will start to drastically improve—if, that is, you truly understand how to engage people in the work you need them to do. When you learn how to do that, when you learn how to replace yourself with other people—people trained in your system—then your practice can really begin to grow. Only then will you begin to experience true freedom yourself.

What typically happens is that accountants, knowing they need help answering the phone, filing, and so on, go out and find someone who can do these things. Once they delegate these duties, however, they rarely spend any time with the employee. Deep down they feel it's not important *how* these things get done; it's only important that they get done.

They fail to grasp the requirement for a system that makes people their greatest asset rather than their greatest liability. A system so reliable that if Chris dropped dead tomorrow, Leslie could do exactly what Chris did. That's where The People Law comes in.

The People Law says that each time you add a new person to your practice using an intelligent (turnkey) system that works, you expand your reach. And you can expand your reach almost infinitely! People allow you to be everywhere you want to be simultaneously, without actually having to be there in the flesh.

People are to an accountant what an album was to Frank Sinatra. A Sinatra record could be (and still is) played in a million places at the same time, regardless of where Frank was. And every record sale produced royalties for Sinatra (or his estate).

With the help of other people, Sinatra created a quality recording that faithfully replicated his unique talents, then made sure it was marketed and distributed, and the revenue managed.

Your people can do the same thing for you. All *you* need to do is to create a "recording"—a system—of your unique talents, your special way of practicing accounting, and then replicate it, market it, distribute it, and manage the revenue.

Isn't that what successful businesspeople do? Make a "recording" of their most effective ways of doing business? In this way, they provide a turnkey solution to their clients' problems. A system solution that really works.

Doesn't your practice offer the same potential for you that records did for Frank Sinatra (and now for his heirs)? The ability to produce income without having to go to work every day?

Isn't that what your people could be for you? The means by which your system for practicing accounting could be faithfully replicated?

But first you've got to have a system. You have to create a unique way of doing business that you can teach to your people, that you can manage faithfully, and that you can replicate consistently, just like McDonald's.

Because without such a system, without such a "recording," without a unique way of doing business that really works, all you're left with is people doing their own thing. And that is almost always a recipe for chaos. Rather than guaranteeing consistency, it encourages mistake after mistake after mistake.

And isn't that how the problem started in the first place? People doing whatever *they* perceived they needed to do, regardless of what you wanted? People left to their own devices, with no regard for the costs of their behavior? The costs to you?

In other words, people without a system.

Can you imagine what would have happened to Frank Sinatra if he had followed that example? If every one who bought one of his recordings ended up with something different? Imagine a million different versions of Frank singing "My Way." It's unthinkable.

Would you buy a record like that? What if Frank was having a bad day? What if he had a sore throat?

Please hear this: The People Law is unforgiving. Without a systematic way of doing business, people are more often a liability than an asset. Unless you prepare, you'll find out too late which ones are which.

The People Law says that, without a specific system for doing business; without a specific system for recruiting, hiring, and training your people to use that system; and without a specific system for managing and improving your systems, your practice will always be a crapshoot.

Do you want to roll the dice with your practice at stake? Unfortunately, that is what most accountants are doing.

The People Law also says that you can't effectively delegate your responsibilities unless you have something specific to delegate. And that something specific is a way of doing business that works!

Frank Sinatra is gone, but his voice lives on. And someone is still counting his royalties. That's because Sinatra had a system that worked.

Do you? Do you get to be as well as to do? Do, be, do, be, do? Or are you just doing, all day long? Now let's move on to the subject of *associate accountants*. But first, let's hear what Darren has to say about *people*.

CHAPTER

10

We the People

M. Darren Root

You're only as good as the people you hire.

—Ray Kroc

When you have the proper systems in place, it's time to assemble the right team of people to manage those systems effectively.

The adage, "There is no *i* in *team*," is as true as ever. Successful firms are supported by a group of dedicated people comprising individuals with varying levels of experience and skill. Savvy business leaders develop the right cadre of employees to ensure their firms run smoothly and processes are followed to the letter.

Far too often I encounter firm leaders who insist on having their hands in every aspect of operations. They hang on to their technician role, unable to break free and relinquish "power" to their staff. This is known as the "me" mentality. In other words, "Without me, things would fall apart." Sound familiar?

Accountants need to get rid of the "me" and adopt a "we" mind-set, where they envision firm operations running independent of their own involvement. It's time to trust your people, let go, and give yourself the opportunity to work on your practice . . . not in it.

One of the first things I want to get clear is that very little performed in our practice requires a CPA or licensed practitioner. Think about it: A license is not required to prepare, assemble, or sign a tax return. A license is not required to prepare payroll, compile information for a set of financial statements, or process payroll tax returns. Because the majority of tasks within your firm do not require certification, you can hand those tasks over to your very competent employees!

Up to this point, you've read about all the work that needs to be done: defining your service offerings and your client base; developing processes and systems; and ensuring you have the appropriate business, practice, and completion plans in place. Now it's time to make sure you have the right people in place to get the work done.

In his bestselling book, *Good to Great,* Jim Collins illustrates this concept by comparing your staff to people on a bus. He said you must not only have the right people on your bus, but they must also be in the right seats. All too often, we have people in the wrong seats—that is, performing tasks that their skills do not support. For example, why would you have a painfully shy person sitting in the reception area tasked with greeting people? When you place an employee in the wrong seat, you set up that person for failure. Thoughtless placement of employees will always result in inefficiency and unrest among staff.

To avoid bad placements, spend adequate time designing job descriptions to ensure a good fit. When you do this, you develop a staff that has a vested interest in the firm's success, because they can easily succeed in their positions.

Creating proper job descriptions is only the first step, however. You must also define your hiring process.

As you may know, hiring the right person requires more than matching skills on a resume to a given position. Candidates not only must possess the right skills but also must be a fit with your culture. You can easily identify skills and experience via a résumé and cover letter. Personality and idiosyncrasies are less easy to assess.

Many accountants are hell-bent on one-on-one interviews, sure that only they have the skills to pick the right candidate. This assumption is a fatal flaw in the hiring process. In fact, group interviews are far more telling and successful when you're selecting a candidate. First, a group interview allows all staff to assess an interviewee. After all, it's your staff who will be working with the new hire on a daily basis. Second, this technique promotes open, casual dialog—and that's when a person's real personality emerges and you can truly assess the potential synergy with your team. In contrast, rarely does an interviewee abandon "show time" mode to show "the real me" during a one-to-one meeting with the head honcho.

After an interview, be sure to reassemble your team and debrief them about the interview. Getting input from everyone is helpful and will bring to light items and issues you may have overlooked. With the proper information in place, you're better equipped to hire the right candidate.

Hiring isn't the end of the process. You still have to invest the proper time in each employee. It's important to spend time with new hires and existing staff, always reminding them of the firm's goals and broad vision and keeping them apprised of system changes. With a solid grasp on their duties and up-to-date knowledge of the firm's strategic trajectory, staff members have a vested interest in the firm's success.

To make sure you have the right people in the right seats, have a plan in place for bringing on new people. That is, you need a *system* for hiring. A firm's hiring system requires one full day of orientation, including:

- An initial new hire meeting with the office administrator to complete appropriate paperwork and provide a detailed explanation of office policies and procedures.
- A meeting with a manager or team leader to explain the firm's vision, working culture, goals, client work, and systems.
- Scheduled time to introduce the employee to the firm's technology, specifically to the tools they'll need to accomplish tasks within their working process. Also make sure employees are fully set up with access and proper logins, and explain the necessity of system security.

A firm's hiring system should also incorporate assignment of a mentor who offers a point of contact (POC) for the new hire. Any new employee is sure to have several questions within the first few weeks while trying to get acclimated to the firm's environment. A dedicated POC offers a new employee a single, knowledgeable, and accessible veteran to provide quick answers.

A mentor will progressively assign projects to the new hire, while explaining the processes (and offering the documentation) that support the tasks. The mentor monitors the new hire's progress, adjusting technique as they go along. For at least the first few months, ensure that the mentor checks in with the new hire to assess progress.

With a system for hiring and training in place, you can get a new team member up to speed and producing in no time. And each time you go through this process, it gets easier.

We've established the need for making good hires. We've also reviewed a system for ensuring that you hire the right people and retain them. Now let's focus on an all-too-common belief among accountants—"If I don't do it, it won't get done right."

Recently, while teaching at a conference in Seattle, I had a debate with a practitioner who simply did not agree with my philosophies on building a business. His stance? He said he was happy being a technician, claiming that if he wanted something done right he needed to do it himself. When I asked him why he had invested his time and money to attend a seminar on becoming a Next Generation Accounting Firm, he replied that he wanted to grow his business and have more time to himself. The irony here is that this practitioner will never grow his business or have more free time if he continues to act as his own primary technician.

I offer this example to highlight the need for a change in mind-set. Accountants can no longer think like technicians, taking on all tasks at every level. A firm *can* and *will* operate without your handprint at each stage of every service process. It can, and more important, it *should*. If accountants want to grow their firms and accomplish true life–work balance, they must build a team to do so.

In my practice, I have designed each of our service offerings so that I have no direct client responsibilities. Every project that leaves the firm is the primary responsibility of one of my dedicated, competent team members. Having the right people in place and entrusting the process to them, I am free to focus on business strategy, including enhancing our technology and processes to ensure my team continues to support our clients effectively (and without me).

Now, a bit about organizational structure. In most firms you have administrative staff, paraprofessionals, professional staff, and partners (you). Administrative staff is usually nonbillable. Therefore, I suggest every nonbillable task within a process be assigned to administrative staff, such as document scanning and collection of client signatures.

For your paraprofessionals, train them to handle as much of the data entry, reconciliations, and requests for client data as possible. Have paraprofessionals develop relationships with clients. It is a positive thing when clients feel comfortable working with multiple people within your firm.

Your professional staff should handle the remainder of the client work, overseeing quality and making sure tasks and projects are completed in a timely manner. Depending on the client type, whether it's bookkeeping, write-up, or payroll, each client should be assigned a team. The team will include at least one paraprofessional and one professional staff member—and neither of these should be you.

It's important to maintain a consistent, positive relationship with each client. Clients need to know they can count on you for quality advice and guidance. However, you shouldn't be the one doing each and every task for clients. Trust your team. You hired them for a reason.

In order to run your practice, design service offerings, and develop and maintain firm systems; you cannot spend your whole day "doing it, doing it, doing it." You must create a buffer from day-to-day work. This is crucial in creating a successful business.

This sounds simple in theory, but I know how difficult it can be to remove that technician's hat. You feel like your clients only want to see and work with you. Also, by the time they've trained an employee to oversee a task, many accountants feel that they could have done the task themselves. Don't think that way if you ever expect to build your business, separate yourself from the minutiae, and obtain true life–work balance.

Get the right people into the right seats on your bus.

On the Subject of Associate Accountants

Michael E. Gerber

Associate yourself with men of good quality if you esteem your own reputation, for 'tis better to be alone than in bad company.
—George Washington

If you're a sole practitioner—that is, you're selling only yourself—then your accounting company called a practice will never make the leap to an accounting company called a business. The progression from practice to business to enterprise demands that you hire other accountants to do what you do (or don't do). Contractors call these people subcontractors; for our purposes, we'll refer to them as associate accountants.

Contractors know that subs can be a huge problem. It's no less true for accountants. Until you face this special business problem, your practice will never become a business, and your business will certainly never become an enterprise.

Long ago, God said, "Let there be accountants. And so they never forget who they are in My creation, let them be damned forever to hire people exactly like themselves." Enter the associates.

Merriam-Webster's Collegiate Dictionary, Eleventh Edition, defines "sub" as "under, below, secretly; inferior to." If associate accountants are like subaccountants, you could define an associate as "an inferior individual contracted to perform part or all of another's contract."

In other words, you, the accountant, make a conscious decision to hire someone "inferior" to you to fulfill *your* commitment to *your* client, for which you are ultimately and solely liable.

Why in the world do we do these things to ourselves? Where will this madness lead? It seems the blind are leading the blind, and the blind are paying others to do it. And when an accountant is blind, you *know* there's a problem!

It's time to step out of the darkness and come into the light. Forget about being Mr. Nice Guy—it's time to do things that work.

Solving the Associate Accountant Problem

Let's say you're about to hire an associate accountant. Someone who has specific skills: audits, multistate taxation, whatever. It all starts with choosing the right personnel. After all, these are people to whom you are delegating your responsibility and for whose behavior you are completely liable. Do you really want to leave that choice to chance? Are you that much of a gambler? I doubt it.

If you've never worked with your new associate, how do you really know the person is skilled? For that matter, what does "skilled" mean?

For you to make an intelligent decision about this associate accountant, you must have a working definition of the word "skilled." Your challenge is to know *exactly* what your expectations are, then to make sure your other accountants operate with precisely the same expectations. Failure here almost assures a breakdown in your relationship.

I want you to write the following on a piece of paper: "By 'skilled,' I mean . . . " Once you create your personal definition of the word, it will become a standard for you and your practice, for your clients, and for your associate accountants.

A "standard," according to *Webster's*, is something "set up and established by authority as a rule for the measure of quantity, weight, extent, value, or quality."

Thus, your goal is to establish a measure of quality control, a standard of skill, which you will apply to all your associate accountants. More important, you are also setting a standard for the performance of your company.

By creating standards for your selection of other accountants—standards of skill, performance, integrity, financial stability, and experience—you have begun the powerful process of building a practice that can operate exactly as you expect it to.

By carefully thinking about exactly what to expect, you have already begun to improve your practice.

In this enlightened state, you will see the selection of your associates as an opportunity to define what you (1) intend to provide for your clients, (2) expect from your employees, and (3) demand for your life.

Powerful stuff, isn't it? Are you up to it? Are you ready to feel your rising power?

Don't rest on your laurels just yet. Defining those standards is only the first step you need to take. The second step is to create an associate accountant development system.

An associate accountant development system is an action plan designed to tell you what you are looking for in an associate. It includes the exact benchmarks, accountabilities, timing of fulfillment, and budget you will assign to the process of looking for associate accountants, identifying them, recruiting them, interviewing them, training them, managing their work, auditing their performance, compensating them, reviewing them regularly, and terminating or rewarding them for their performance.

All of these things must be documented—actually *written down*—if they're going to make any difference to you, your associate accountants, your managers, or your bank account!

And then you've got to persist with that system, come hell or high water. Just as Ray Kroc did. Just as Walt Disney did. Just as Sam Walton did.

This leads us to our next topic of discussion: the subject of *estimating*. But first, let's listen to what Darren has to say on the subject of *associate accountants*.

CHAPTER 12

Building a Professional Team

M. Darren Root

Nothing is particularly hard if you divide it into small jobs.

—Henry Ford

I n this chapter, you'll learn about the necessity of building your professional team. Your team is the group of individuals you count on to manage operations—whether you are there or not. Members of your professional team also take on the role of go-to person for clients and your core employees.

Savvy business leaders understand the importance of building a strong team and dividing work proportionately and appropriately, based on skill sets. With the right players on board (this includes the right blend of your licensed and core team members), no amount of client work is too much. Your staff, in essence, represents a system within a system—moving work seamlessly through your firm.

Let's consider the common makeup of today's small to mid-size accounting firm.

Depending on your service offerings, your firm may or may not employ licensed professionals. If your practice is one that prepares audits or performs consulting work, you most assuredly have licensed staff. If your practice consists largely of bookkeeping, write-up, and payroll services, which don't require a licensed professional to perform, you may not.

In either case, if you operate a firm in which you are the only licensed professional, it's safe to assume that your entire staff consists of administrative employees and paraprofessionals. It's also safe to assume that you are the go-to person for all employees and clients—and that makes it very difficult to get out from under the myriad tasks associated with being the firm's sole technician.

I talk to many accountants, and a fair number insist that growth is not their main focus. In fact, they prefer to stay small.

That is all well and good. But growth is not the only benefit of turning your firm into a business. What about flexibility and balance with your personal life? Not to mention simply eliminating the tedium and stress of perpetually dealing with daily operational tasks. When you are the only licensed professional on staff, you are the one doing all the work—hindering your ability to achieve life–work balance and forever keeping you chained to day-to-day operations.

Since implementing the principles of the E-Myth in my own firm, one of my greatest achievements is freedom. I have the right professionals in place to handle daily operations, so I can enjoy working on my business . . . or just being away from the office now and then.

At some point, you have to ask yourself, "Do I want to do it all myself?" If your answer is "No," then hiring one or more professional staff members is probably in your future. If you already have licensed staff, it may be time to reevaluate how you're using them.

Growing Your Firm Doesn't Necessarily Mean Hiring More Staff

There's a common misconception about the relationship between growth and professional staff. People often think of growth as directly related to the number of professionals hired. Accountants believe that the more billable-hour resources you have available, the more billings you can achieve. In other words, the bigger you get, the more staff you require.

Not true.

The old business model has long been to sell billable hours. The problem with this model is that the only way to increase revenue is to increase the number of billable hours available. With this model, all you end up doing is working more hours and hiring more staff—without any notable revenue growth.

But there's another option. Assume that the billable hour is not your primary "product." Instead of selling billable hours, your firm sells complete solutions. One solution could be a tax return. Other solutions could be a monthly compilation report or an annual audit. These solutions have a perceived value to you and your clients. You sell this solution at a fee that supports the value.

If your goal is to get off the proverbial hamster wheel and build a business, it is critical to abandon the billable-hour model and adopt value billing. The value-billing model allows you to continually develop solutions to sell at a set fee, instead of billing more hours and expanding professional staff beyond what you really need.

The Importance of Building a Professional Team

So far, this book has encouraged you to think about the type business you want to develop, define your services, develop the right systems, and commit a plan in writing. We've also discussed getting the right people in the right seats on the bus. All of these concepts are significant in building your business, but I cannot overstate the importance of building your professional team.

Without the proper professional team in place, you're left managing service offerings and all the duties that go with being the central go-to person. Essentially, you can kiss any freedom goodbye.

So how do you know when you need to hire a professional, and who's the right professional to hire?

Before we venture into hiring, now is a good time to recall the importance of systems.

Before you can even think about hiring a licensed staff member, you must make sure that your core team is in place in order to support a well-established workflow system. In Chapter 10, I discussed the necessity of creating a solid team . . . getting the right people in the right positions. When your core team is in place, and when you've defined the tasks assigned to each of these employees, you're in a better position to define the duties of your professional staff.

Having an established core team also means that your professional staff will be properly supported from the start, and your overall workflow system will continue to run smoothly. In a proper system, your administrative employees handle all administrative work and your paraprofessionals take care of routine client work. The last thing you want is for your professional staff conducting administrative work. What a waste of time!

When and How to Hire Professional Staff

One of the easiest ways to determine whether you require additional licensed staff is to take an honest look at your own workload. With your current workload, do you have time to research and deploy new technologies, help staff members learn and grow, and plan the strategic direction of your firm? Additionally, are you able to take time away from the office and do the things you enjoy? If most of your honest answers are "No," it's time to hire.

As we all know, hiring the "right" person can be tricky. Chapter 10's tips on hiring also apply to professional staff. Allow your entire team to interview candidates, look for personality and culture fit along with experience and skills, and so on.

To further prepare yourself for hiring the right person, it is critical that you define the roles and responsibilities of the position *before* you enter the hiring process. Create a proper job description so you know what to look for and so the interviewee knows what's expected of him or her. You can't expect to hire the right person if no one knows the position's specifics and expectations.

As Chapter 10 also emphasizes, you need to provide proper training. Your hiring system must support focused, precise training of new professional team members. Training should include an overview of the position's required duties, detailed instruction on your firm's structured processes for workflow, and the technology solutions that deliver client services and support internal systems.

And don't forget about mentoring. You or one of your other professional staff members will serve as a mentor for new hires. As new professional staff become acclimated to your firm's culture and work processes, you can slowly transition the management of clients from your plate to theirs.

At the end of the day, developing a solid professional team takes you one big step closer to achieving some real balance between working and living. Handing over some of what has probably become a crippling amount of work is the key to your own personal freedom.

CHAPTER 13

On the Subject of Estimating

Michael E. Gerber

*The way a chihuahua goes about eating a dead elephant is to take
a bite and be very present with that bite. In spiritual growth, the
definitive act is to take one step and let tomorrow's step take care
of itself.*

—William H. Houff, *Infinity in Your Hand:
A Guide for the Spiritually Curious*

O ne of the greatest weaknesses of accountants is accurately estimating how long services will take and
then scheduling their clients accordingly. *Webster's
Collegiate Dictionary* defines "estimate" as "a rough or approximate

calculation." Anyone who has visited an accountant's office knows that those estimates can be rough indeed.

Do you want to see someone who gives you a rough approximation? What if your accountant gave you a rough approximation of your company's financial condition?

The fact is that we can predict many things we don't typically predict. For example, there are ways to learn the truth about the tax situation for businesses, couples, and individuals. Look at the steps of the process. Most of the things you do are standard, so develop a step-by-step system and stick to it.

In my book *The E-Myth Manager*, I raised eyebrows by suggesting that medical doctors eliminate the waiting room. Why? You don't need it if you're always on time. The same goes for an accounting practice. If you're always on time, then your clients don't have to go on extension.

What if an accountant made this promise: your return filed on time, every time, as promised, or we pay for it.

"Impossible!" accountants cry. "Each client is different. We simply can't know how long each service will take."

Do you follow this? Since accountants believe they're incapable of knowing how to organize their time, they build a practice based on lack of knowing and lack of control. They build a practice based on estimates.

I once had an accountant ask me, "What happens when someone comes in for a routine planning appointment and we discover that IRS agents are about to conduct a field audit at their offices? How can we deal with something so unexpected? How can we give proper service and stay on schedule?"

The solution is interest, attention, analysis. Try detailing what you do at the beginning of an interaction, what you do in the middle, and what you do at the end. How long does each take? In the absence of such detailed, quantified standards, everything ends up being an estimate, and a poor estimate at that.

However, a practice organized around a system, with adequate staff to run it, has time for proper attention. It's built right into the system.

Too many accountants have grown accustomed to thinking in terms of estimates without thinking about what the term really means. Is it any wonder many accounting practices are in trouble?

Enlightened accountants, in contrast, banish the word *estimate* from their vocabulary. When it comes to estimating, just say no!

"But you can never be exact," accountants have told me for years. "Close, maybe. But never exact."

I have a simple answer to that: *You have to be.* You simply can't afford to be inexact. You can't accept inexactness in yourself or in your accounting practice.

You can't go to work every day believing that your practice, the work you do, and the commitments you make are all too complex and unpredictable to be exact. With a mind-set like that, you're doomed to run a sloppy ship. A ship that will eventually sink and suck you down with it.

This is so easy to avoid. Sloppiness—in both thought and action—is the root cause of your frustrations.

The solution to those frustrations is clarity. Clarity gives you the ability to set a clear direction, which fuels the momentum you need to grow your business.

Clarity, direction, momentum—they all come from insisting on exactness.

But how do you create exactness in a hopelessly inexact world? The answer is: *You discover the exactness in your practice by refusing to do any work that can't be controlled exactly.*

The only other option is to analyze the market, determine where the opportunities are, and then organize your practice to be the exact provider of the services you've chosen to offer.

Two choices, and only two choices: (1) Evaluate your practice and then limit yourself to the tasks you know you can do exactly, or (2) start all over by analyzing the market, identifying the key opportunities in that market, and building a practice that operates exactly.

What you cannot do, what you must refuse to do, from this day forward, is to allow yourself to operate with an inexact mind-set. It will lead you to ruin.

Which leads us inexorably back to the word I have been using throughout this book: *systems*.

Who makes estimates? Only accountants who are unclear about exactly how to do the task in question. Only accountants whose experience has taught them that if something can go wrong, it will—and to them!

I'm not suggesting that a systems solution will guarantee that you always perform exactly as promised. But I am saying that a systems solution will faithfully alert you when you're going off track, and will do it before you have to pay the price for it.

In short, with a systems solution in place, your need to estimate will be a thing of the past, both because you have organized your practice to anticipate mistakes and because you have put in place the system to do something about those mistakes before they blow up.

There's this, too: To make a promise you intend to keep places a burden on you and your managers to dig deeply into how you intend to keep it. Such a burden will transform your intentions and increase your attention to detail.

With the promise will come dedication. With dedication will come integrity. With integrity will come consistency. With consistency will come results you can count on. And results you can count on mean that you get exactly what you hoped for at the outset of your practice: the true pride of ownership that every accountant should experience.

This brings us to the subject of *clients*. Who are they? Why do they come to you? How can you identify yours? And who *should* your clients be? But first, let's listen to what Darren has to say about *estimating*.

The Value of Pricing

M. Darren Root

Pricing should get as much executive commitment and attention as purchasing.

—Ronald J. Baker

The terms value pricing, fixed-price agreements, and fixed fees have all been used in the profession for many years. Yet the thought of abandoning cost-plus pricing and the billable hour is scary for most accountants.

Ron Baker, noted author and the visionary behind the notion of value pricing, has been spreading the word among professional service firms: Value pricing a service is far superior to relying on the traditional cost-plus method and old-fashioned timesheets. And finally, accountants are starting to listen.

Firms have been using a value-based model for years. Think about it. Many have long used flat-fee billing for individual income tax returns. Some firms even bill by the number of forms prepared. Many large accounting firms that perform audits guarantee a fixed fee in their engagement letters.

Realizing that the fixed-price model has been in use for a long time, what is it about the value-pricing model that worries some accountants?

I've never understood the logic behind billing engagements by the hour. Hourly billing does not take into consideration the efficiency of a particular staff member or the technologies that support the process. And in clients' eyes, the hourly billing structure has historically been a major source of irritation. When clients visit your office, call, or e-mail, they know they are "on the clock." This sometimes creates frustration and pushes the client to search for answers independently. Such a situation is not good for the client or the accountant, and it certainly fails to strengthen the professional relationship.

I have long been a proponent of fixed-fee or value pricing. I like the concept of providing clients up front with an explanation of services and the fixed cost. It also expedites the agreement process.

Whether my firm is providing bookkeeping, write-up, or payroll, or preparing tax returns, my staff and I have logged enough experience collectively to create an equitable fixed fee for each service.

The systems a firm has in place and market experience are the keys to being able to develop a fixed-fee model with confidence.

In my firm, given our streamlined processes and advanced integrated technology solutions, we know we can deliver any of our services at a realization greater than 100 percent. Our experience tells us how much time it will take to provide each service. We can also benchmark the value of our services based on what other, comparable firms in our community offer. This intelligence allows us to set a price commensurate with value.

Value pricing allows accountants to take on the role of trusted advisor to their clients, because it frees them from tedious time-tracking. This model also alleviates clients' concern about being billed for every phone call or e-mail.

I am not a proponent of completely throwing out the time-sheet. Tracking time still has a purpose in relation to benchmarking and goals. Take, for example, one issue associated with the fixed-fee arrangement called "scope creep." Scope creep occurs when a client starts injecting additional projects and needs into your fixed agreement after the fixed fee has been determined. Added projects mean added time for the firm.

Tracking time against your fixed-fee engagements allows you to identify scope creep and adjust price accordingly. Tracking time can also help you monitor the efficiency of staff members and coach them to work more efficiently.

Practice Management Systems

Today's advanced practice management systems allow firms to transform manual workflow into an automated electronic process and easily track and monitor projects within advanced dashboards.

For example, the process to complete a 1040 client can be completely automated. Each step of the workflow can be tracked within a practice management system so that, at any time, a partner can pinpoint where a particular staff member is in the process. The system essentially creates a daily tasks list for each employee, keeping them on task to complete the project and bill. Staff time is tracked in real time, offering a clear picture of realization on every engagement.

Becoming Your Clients' Most Trusted Advisor

Firms need to abandon what many clients view as a nickel-and-dime practice of billing. Charging for every single interaction is time-consuming and frustrating to clients. And more often than not it's one too many of the small invoices that puts a client over the edge and drives them to the competition.

Fixed-fee agreements help level out your cash flow and increase client satisfaction. Put yourself in your client's shoes for a moment. Do you feel better when you are buying goods or services knowing up front how much you are going to spend? Of course you do—and so will your clients.

Eliminate the surprise of the monthly invoice and allow your clients to budget their accounting costs for the year. It provides the client with peace of mind.

Do everything possible to create a level of certainty in each client's mind. Help your clients to see you as a partner and, most important, as their most trusted business advisor. Build your business around systems, predictability, consistency, and efficiency. Value pricing will help you achieve these goals.

CHAPTER 15

On the Subject of Clients

Michael E. Gerber

I don't build in order to have clients. I have clients in order to build.
—Ayn Rand

When it comes to the practice of accounting, the best definition of clients I've ever heard is this:

Clients: very special people who drive most accountants crazy.

Does that work for you?

After all, it's a rare client who shows any appreciation for what an accountant has to go through to do the job as promised. Don't clients always think the price is too high? And don't they focus on problems, broken promises, and the mistakes they think you make, rather than all the ways you bend over backward to give them what they need?

Do you ever hear other accountants voice these complaints? More to the point, have you ever voiced them yourself? Well, you're not alone. I have yet to meet an accountant who doesn't suffer from a strong case of client confusion.

Client confusion is about:

- What your client really wants
- How to communicate effectively with your client
- How to keep your client truly happy
- How to deal with client dissatisfaction
- Whom to call a clientele

Confusion 1: What Does Your Client Really Want?

Your clients aren't just people; they're very specific kinds of people. Let me share with you the six categories of clients as seen from the E-Myth marketing perspective:

1. Tactile clients
2. Neutral clients
3. Withdrawal clients
4. Experimental clients
5. Transitional clients
6. Traditional clients

Your entire marketing strategy must be based on which type of client you are dealing with. Each of the six client types spends money on accounting services for very different, and identifiable, reasons. These are:

1. Tactile clients get their major gratification from interacting with other people.

2. Neutral clients get their major gratification from interacting with inanimate objects (computers, cars, information).

3. Withdrawal clients get their major gratification from interacting with ideas (thoughts, concepts, stories).

4. Experimental clients rationalize their buying decisions by perceiving that what they bought is new, revolutionary, and innovative.

5. Transitional clients rationalize their buying decisions by perceiving that what they bought is dependable and reliable.

6. Traditional clients rationalize their buying decisions by perceiving that what they bought is cost-effective, a good deal, and worth the money.

In short:

1. If your client is tactile, you have to emphasize the *people* of your practice.

2. If your client is neutral, you have to emphasize the *technology* of your practice.

3. If your client is a withdrawal client, you have to emphasize the *idea* of your practice.

4. If your client is an experimental client, you have to emphasize the *uniqueness* of your practice.

5. If your client is transitional, you have to emphasize the *dependability* of your practice.

6. If your client is traditional, you have to talk about the *financial competitiveness* of your practice.

What your clients want is determined by who they are. Who they are is regularly demonstrated by what they do. Think about the clients with whom you do business. Ask yourself: In which of the categories would I place each? What does each do for a living?

If your client is a mechanical engineer, for example, it's probably safe to assume he's a neutral client. If another one of your clients is a cardiologist, she's probably tactile. If your client is a power company, it's most likely Transitional, and so are the people who manage it. And software engineers are often experimental.

Having an idea about which categories your clients may fall into is very helpful to figuring out what they want. Of course, there's no exact science to it, and human beings constantly defy stereotypes. So don't take my word for it. You'll want to make your own analysis of the clients you serve.

Confusion 2: How to Communicate Effectively with Your Client

The next step in the client satisfaction process is to decide how to magnify the characteristics of your practice that are most likely to appeal to your preferred category of client. That begins with what marketing people call your positioning strategy.

What do I mean by *positioning* your practice? You position your practice with words—specifically, a few well-chosen words to tell your clients exactly what they want to hear. In marketing lingo, those words are called your USP, or unique selling proposition.

For example, if you are targeting tactile clients (ones who love people), your USP could be: "Martland Accounting, where our people care about our clients!"

If you are targeting experimental clients (ones who love new, revolutionary things), your USP could be: "Martland Accounting, one step ahead of the IRS!" In other words, when they choose to schedule an appointment with you, they can count on both your services and your research and filing technology to be on the cutting edge of the accounting industry.

Is this starting to make sense? Do you see how the ordinary things most accountants do to get clients can be done in a significantly more effective way?

Once you understand the essential principles of marketing the E-Myth way, the strategies by which you attract clients can make an enormous difference in your market share.

Confusion 3: How to Keep Your Client Happy

Let's say you've overcome the first two sources of confusion. Great. Now how do you keep your client happy?

Very simple . . . just keep your promise! And make sure your client *knows* you kept your promise every step of the way.

In short, giving your clients what they think they want is the key to keeping your clients (or anyone else, for that matter) really happy.

If your clients need to interact with people (high touch, tactile), make certain that they do.

If they need to interact with things (high tech, neutral), make certain that they do.

If they need to interact with ideas (in their head, withdrawal), make certain that they do.

And so forth.

At E-Myth, we call this your client fulfillment system. It's the step-by-step process by which you do the task you've contracted to do and deliver what you've promised—on time, every time.

But what happens when your clients are *not* happy? What happens when you've done everything I've mentioned here and your client is still dissatisfied?

Confusion 4: How to Deal with Client Dissatisfaction

If you have followed each step up to this point, client dissatisfaction will be rare. But it can and will still occur—people are people, and some people will always find a way to be dissatisfied with something. Here's what to do about it:

1. Always listen to what your clients are saying. And never interrupt while they're saying it.

2. After you're sure you've heard all of your client's complaint, make absolutely certain you understand what she said by phrasing a question such as: "Can I repeat what you've just told me, Ms. Harton, to make absolutely certain I understand you?"

3. Secure your client's acknowledgment that you have heard her complaint accurately.

4. Apologize for whatever your client thinks you did that dissatisfied her . . . even if you didn't do it!

5. After your client has acknowledged your apology, ask her exactly what would make her happy.

6. Repeat what your client told you would make her happy, and get her acknowledgment that you have heard correctly.

7. If at all possible, give your client exactly what she has asked for.

You may be thinking, "But what if my client wants something totally impossible?" Don't worry. If you've followed my recommendations to the letter, what your client asks for will seldom seem unreasonable.

Confusion 5: Whom to Call a Client

At this stage, it's important to ask yourself some questions about the kind of clients you hope to attract to your practice:

- Which types of clients would you most like to do business with?
- Where do you see your real market opportunities?
- Whom would you like to work with, provide services to, and position your business for?

In short, *it's all up to you*. No mystery. No magic. Just a systematic process for shaping your practice's future. But you must have the passion to pursue the process. And you must be absolutely clear about every aspect of it.

Until you know your clients as well as you know yourself.

Until all your complaints about clients are a thing of the past.

Until you accept the undeniable fact that client acquisition and client satisfaction are more science than art.

But unless you're willing to grow your practice, you better not follow any of these recommendations. Because if you do what I'm suggesting, it's going to grow.

This brings us to the subject of *growth*. But first, let's listen to what Darren has to say about *clients*.

CHAPTER 16

Making It All about the Client

M. Darren Root

To be trusted is a greater compliment than to be loved.
—George MacDonald

S o far, we've spent a lot of time talking about systems, processes, and staff. Of course, these things are of little importance if you don't have clients. Our clients enable us to grow and move forward. They are our greatest assets.

The client–accountant relationship is special—one built on an immense level of trust. Clients depend on us to be their trusted advisor, providing so much more than delivery of financial statements or tax returns. Clients look to their accountant for sage business advice to ensure business and personal success.

No doubt many of you have been approached with such questions as these: Should I refinance my house? Can I afford a new piece of equipment? How does my business look compared to others? From time to time, you may get frustrated with all the questions that come your way, but such is life for a client's most trusted business advisor. The bottom line is that the relationship between the accountant and the client is considered a special bond—one that we should cherish.

Our clients are different from those within many other professions. Due to the recurring nature of our work, we develop closer relationships with clients and are not burdened with the constant necessity of acquiring new clients to build a successful business. As the work recurs, clients are also recurring, and as such represent a perpetual revenue stream and long-term business.

Consider a few examples of recurring relationships. Payroll clients recur weekly or biweekly, while other accounting clients are on a monthly or quarterly basis. Even our annual clients are recurring, providing an opportunity for ongoing work. In each of these scenarios, clients are part of a cyclical process that keeps those clients in our office and on our books.

The Necessity of Positive Clients

Despite the built-in recurring nature of accounting work, it's important to emphasize that client relationships should never be taken for granted. It's easy to get into the habit of simply delivering product, while overlooking opportunities to enhance client relations. Are you guilty of this? Ask yourself, "When was the last time I worked on building client relationships?" If it's been a while, you may be missing out on some real growth opportunities.

When most accountants talk about practice building, they are really referring to obtaining new clients. In fact, developing a steady stream of new clients is typically the sole focus of their marketing efforts. And while new client acquisition is part of a sound business model, maintaining existing clients is even more important to business growth. Think about it:

- Setting up new clients is far more time-consuming (and therefore initially less profitable) than maintaining your existing client base.

- Focusing on selling value-added services to current clients offers the opportunity to increase revenue quickly. And the more services a client procures, the "stickier" they become.

- Dedicating ample time to client-relation activity helps to develop a strong bond between client and trusted advisor— helping to foster a long-term business relationship.

- Focusing on bringing in new clients takes away from ongoing client-relation efforts. The result is often the loss of existing clients, which means you only have to work harder to bring in more new clients. It's a vicious circle.

It makes sense to work steadily on strengthening relationships with existing clients, while simultaneously working to add clients who fit your target client demographic.

Our current clients represent a gold mine of future opportunities. So as part of your core system, you should assign someone in your office to spend time analyzing your existing clients' needs. Thorough and consistent analysis will help you identify areas where you can help your clients succeed—and sometimes that means added services.

As part of the evaluation, ask such questions as:

- Are your clients working as efficiently as they could be?
- Are they using the latest and best technologies to run their businesses?
- Do they have the appropriate systems and processes in place to create their ideal business?
- Does the client require additional accounting services to make their working lives easier?

The answers to these questions will not only help your clients; they may result in additional revenue streams for your firm.

When I first started out in practice, I asked a friend who had a successful law practice how he did it. I've operated my practice based on his response. What he said was this: Listen to your clients, treat them as friends, and do what you say you're going to do. This advice has served me well, so I pass it on to you along with what I've learned along the way:

- First, clients want to be heard, so listen to them and try and understand what they want from you. This is where performing regular evaluations of client accounts is incredibly valuable. Through a true understanding of needs, you can provide the perfect solution and maintain clients far longer.
- Second, clients look to their accountant to solve their problems. We are in the problem-solving business. I always tell my staff that if our clients cease to have problems and questions, then we are out of business. So, help clients identify where they may be having issues and work to develop resolutions.
- Third, our clients want to be led. We are the professionals, so we need to invest the time to lead our clients in the direction they should go, the direction that is best for them.

Whether it's technology needs, business-process improvement, or financial advice, we must lead the client toward success.

With all this information in mind, devote a good portion of your marketing budget to initiatives geared toward strengthening existing client relationships. Put the remainder of the budget toward activity surrounding new-client acquisition. As discussed, it's much easier and more profitable to invest in existing clients than to market for new ones. Consider the following:

- The cost of attracting a new client is 5 to 12 times greater than the cost of retaining an existing client.
- ROI for client-retention activities is 10 times higher than for new-client marketing.
- Existing clients can be the best source of new client referrals, out-producing even the best marketing efforts.
- Leveraging the potential of existing clients quickly increases bottom-line profits.

Based on these statistics, it makes sense that firms should have a sound communications program in place for existing clients. Good, consistent communication is probably the single most important factor in maintaining clients in the long term.

When I ask new clients who come to my firm why they left their previous accountant, the answer is often lack of communication. If we are not keeping in contact with our clients, we are not doing our jobs. Communication is crucial.

The best communication advice I can offer is this: Be responsive. E-mail and call clients back in a timely manner. Often, a client is waiting for answers from you before she can move forward in her own work. Fast, reliable communication is the key to maintaining clients.

Another way to create a strong communications program is to reach out on a regular basis. This can be accomplished via a dedicated client newsletter, e-mail blasts that contain timely and helpful information, informational lunch meetings, holiday cards, or client appreciation events. Each of these communication vehicles represents a consistent touch point that helps build stronger relationships.

Every communication initiative mentioned here offers an opportunity to get to know clients and for them to get to know you. Accountants get a bad rap. We're often thought of as uncommunicative, boring, and having little personality. Obviously, this stereotype is untrue. By hosting events or providing other communications like newsletters, you have the opportunity to showcase your personality and make a positive impression on clients and prospects.

Understanding Client Types

As Michael mentioned in Chapter 15, there are many different kinds of clients. He categorizes them as tactile, neutral, withdrawal, experimental, transitional, and traditional. To market and communicate to clients and prospects effectively, you must understand the various client types. You also must know which types you and your staff are best equipped to serve . . . and *want* to serve.

For example, I often hear from colleagues, "My clients won't have anything to do with computers or the Internet." Although this may be true for a small cadre of clients, you must understand your broad client base in order to maintain existing clients and acquire new ones who best fit to your business. For example, if you have a large number of neutral clients—those who get their major gratification from interacting with objects (like computers)—your practice should support an advanced technology platform for service delivery.

Identifying your mix of clients is, of course, a complex activity. You will have some clients who fall into several categories and others who fall into only one. You can see the importance, however, of knowing your client base in order to support their needs with appropriate systems, services, and communication.

As Michael also mentioned in Chapter 15, building a proper communication strategy will help you effectively reach your preferred client types. For example, if you are meeting with a prospect who is a physician and you know the prospect falls into the neutral category, is very busy, and wants services performed accurately and on time, then you want to emphasize your firm's use of technology and structured processes. You also want to identify the value of your delivery platform, that is, the convenience and efficiency offered to the client. You can emphasize the ability to access documents in real time via the Web, the timeliness of file delivery, and so on.

Your client base is your firm's biggest asset, and maintaining current clients is the fastest, easiest way to grow your business and increase revenue. Clients represent a referral gold mine, and they can provide additional revenue streams through value-added services. It's important to maintain a sound client-relations program to keep your clients happy—and to keep recurring revenue coming into your firm. Marketing communications efforts are essential to maintain positive communication with existing clients and to acquire new ones. The bottom line: Treat your clients right, and you'll be rewarded many times over.

CHAPTER 17

On the Subject of Growth

Michael E. Gerber

Growth is the only evidence of life.
—John Henry Newman, *Apologia Pro Vita Sua*

The rule of business growth says that every business, like every child, is destined to grow. Needs to grow. Is determined to grow.

Once you've created your accounting practice, once you've shaped the idea of it, the most natural thing for it to do is to . . . *grow*! And if you stop it from growing, it will die.

Once an accountant has started a practice, it's his or her job to help it grow. To nurture it and support it in every way. To infuse it with these qualities:

- Purpose
- Passion

- Will
- Belief
- Personality
- Method

As your practice grows, it naturally changes. And as it changes from a small practice to something much bigger, you will begin to feel out of control. News flash: That's because you *are* out of control.

Your practice has exceeded your know-how, sprinted right past you, and now it's taunting you to keep up. That leaves you two choices: Grow as big as your practice demands you to grow, or try to hold your practice at its present level—the level where you feel most comfortable.

The sad fact is that most accountants do the latter. They try to keep their practice small, securely within their comfort zone. Doing what they know how to do, what they feel most comfortable doing. It's called playing it safe.

But as the practice grows, the number, scale, and complexity of tasks will grow, too, until they threaten to overwhelm the accountant. More people are needed. More space. More money. Everything seems to be happening at the same time. A hundred balls are in the air at once.

As I've said throughout this book: Most accountants are not entrepreneurs. They aren't true businesspeople at all, but technicians suffering from an entrepreneurial seizure. Their philosophy of coping with the workload can be summarized as "just do it," rather than figuring out how to get it done through other people, using innovative systems to produce consistent results.

Given most accountants' inclination to be the master juggler in their practice, it's not surprising that as complexity increases, as work expands beyond their ability to do it, as money becomes more elusive, they are just holding on, desperately juggling more and more balls. In the end, most collapse under the strain.

You can't expect your practice to stand still. You can't expect your practice to stay small. A practice that stays small and depends on you to do everything isn't a practice—it's a job!

Yes, just like your children, your business must be allowed to grow, to flourish, to change, to become more than it is. In this way, it will match your vision. And you know all about vision, right? You better. It's what an entrepreneur does best!

Do you feel the excitement? You should. After all, you know what your practice is but not what it can be.

It's either going to grow or die. The choice is yours, but it is a choice that must be made. If you sit back and wait for change to overtake you, you will always have to answer "No" to this question: Are you ready?

This brings us to the subject of *change*. But first, let's listen to what Darren has to say about *growth*.

CHAPTER 18

The Art of Growth

M. Darren Root

The great thing in the world is not so much where we stand, as in what direction we are moving.

—Oliver Wendell Holmes, Sr.

Without growth, we stagnate. A business that is not growing is declining; that is true. However, not all growth is good. In fact, growth for the sake of growth can be harmful.

Everything we have discussed so far has been designed to help you grow your practice. The intent of this chapter is not to contradict previous statements. Growth is positive. However, growing your practice the right way is an art. If you can master the art of healthy growth, you will find you are moving in the right direction.

Accountants typically fall into one of two camps in relation to growing their practices:

- Camp 1 relies primarily on consistently acquiring new clients. Being in this camp, which is typically made up of technicians, can be exhausting.
- Camp 2 relies on enhancing systems to increase efficiency, which allows for growth in client base without adding resources. Being in this camp is far more relaxing; it's made up of savvy business leaders.

If you've been building your practice for some time, you may have reached a crossroad—wondering whether you are running your business or your business is running you. Because you're reading this book, my guess is that you are ready to change direction—a direction that will stop you from "doing it, doing it, doing it" . . . like those in Camp 1.

Although your business is very personal, it's an entity that should be able to stand on its own. A friend and business partner once told me that I needed to look at my own firm as if it sat under a glass dome. What he was trying to convey was that my accounting firm was a unique entity that's separate from me. The metaphor of the dome signified my ability to view my business from above, where I could comfortably plan, design, and strategize. I could be in charge, but still be separate.

Like most practitioners, I have an innate urge to be under the glass, to be inside and attached to my firm, entrenched in its day-to-day operations. But that's a technician's mentality. As your practice grows, it's helpful to visualize the glass dome so you can understand the necessity of staying out of the administrative minutiae and leading your firm from a higher place. That's the message from Camp 2!

Technology and Growth

For those who have graduated to Camp 2, technology is central. And today, more tested, proven technology solutions are available to the accounting profession than ever before. When you apply the right set of tools intelligently, you can create the processes and systems required to run a highly efficient business—one that can continue to take on new clients at a much greater rate and without the associated "peoplepower."

Advanced technology and automation solutions are no longer a luxury to be implemented by a select few. Technology is broadly available and a necessity for all firms—large and small. If you want to survive and thrive in today's environment, you must embrace, learn, and implement technology. Use technology to automate routine tasks, implement paperless workflows, provide client portals for real-time product delivery, and utilize powerful practice management systems that support up-to-the-minute tracking of every engagement.

Think about it: The more time it takes to perform routine tasks, the greater the cost to the firm. The time savings offered by automating processes equates to big money. Time saved can go toward performing additional value-added services for clients, opening up a world of opportunity to generate more revenue.

To use technology effectively, you must think about technology in a new way. Many accountants I talk to think of technology as an expense, when it should be considered an investment. If you invest in an application that saves staff significant hours of billable time, it's a good investment. To build your business, you must understand technology: how to apply it, its advantages, and how to integrate it throughout your firm to create seamless and highly efficient workflow processes.

Social Media and Growth

Facebook, Twitter, and LinkedIn are all excellent social media channels that have made it exceptionally easy to reach current and future clients—and have them reach you. When I give a presentation, I always ask attendees how they find products. Their answer is always "the Internet." Clients are finding services the same way, so if you don't have a presence on the Web, how do you expect people to find you?

Social media, like any other kind of communication we've discussed, is an opportunity to put your best foot forward and make a positive impression. Your social media sites require dedicated investment. Make sure your look is consistent with your brand, your posts are thoughtful, and you are consistent in your message. You should always feel confident to send people to your social media sites, just as you would your web site.

Technologies for the accounting profession are more abundant than at any other point in history. We've come a long way. I still remember helping my father in his firm—using carbon paper between two forms to make copies and manually writing clients' names and Social Security numbers on forms. Those days are gone, thank goodness! Firms have to get on board with available technology. Although becoming technologically savvy may seem overwhelming, trust that it's not nearly as overwhelming as performing tasks manually. Technology is a friend to the profession and at the heart of how smart business leaders are artfully growing their firms. It's time to adapt.

CHAPTER 19

On the Subject of Change

Michael E. Gerber

All change implies loss, and loss must be mourned.
—M. Scott Peck, *The Road Less Traveled*

S o your practice is growing. That means, of course, that it's also changing. Which means it's driving you and everyone in your life crazy.

To most people, change is a diabolical thing. Tell most people they've got to change, and their first instinct is to crawl directly into a hole. Nothing threatens their existence more than change. Nothing cements their resistance more than change. Nothing.

Yet for the past 35 years, that's exactly what I've been proposing to small-business owners: the need to change. Not for the sake of change itself, but for the sake of their lives.

I've talked to countless accountants whose hopes weren't being realized through their practice; whose lives were consumed by work; who slaved increasingly longer hours for decreasing pay; whose dissatisfaction grew as their enjoyment shriveled; whose practice had become the worst job in the world; whose money was out of control; whose employees were a source of never-ending hassles, just like their clients, their bank, and, increasingly, even their family.

More and more, these accountants spent their time alone, dreading the unknown and anxious about the future. And even when they were with people, they didn't know how to relax. Their mind was always on the job. They were distracted by work, by the thought of work. By the fear of falling behind.

And yet, when confronted with their condition and offered an alternative, most of the same accountants strenuously resisted. They assumed that if there were a better way of doing business, they already would have figured it out. They derived comfort from knowing what they believed they already knew. They accepted the limitations of being an accountant; or the truth about people; or the limitations of what they could expect from their clients, their employees, their associate accountants, their bankers—even their family and friends.

In short, most accountants I've met over the years would rather live with the frustrations they already have than risk enduring new frustrations.

Isn't that true of most people you know? Rather than opening up to the infinite number of possibilities life offers, they prefer to shut their lives down to respectable limits. After all, isn't that the most reasonable way to live?

I think not. I think we must learn to let go. I think that if you fail to embrace change, it will inevitably destroy you.

Conversely, by opening yourself to change, you give your accounting practice the opportunity to get the most from your talents.

Let me share with you an original way to think about change, about life, about who we are and what we do. About the stunning notion of expansion and contraction.

Contraction versus Expansion

"Our salvation," a wise man once said, "is to allow," that is, to be open, to let go of our beliefs, to change. Only then can we move from a point of view to a viewing point.

That wise man was Thaddeus Golas, the author of a small, powerful book titled *The Lazy Man's Guide to Enlightenment* (Seed Center, 1971).

Among the many inspirational things he had to say was this compelling idea:

> *The basic function of each being is expanding and contracting. Expanded beings are permeative; contracted beings are dense and impermeative. Therefore each of us, alone or in combination, may appear as space, energy, or mass, depending on the ratio of expansion to contraction chosen, and what kind of vibrations each of us expresses by alternating expansion and contraction. Each being controls his own vibrations.*

In other words, Golas tells us that the entire mystery of life can be summed up in two words: *expansion* and *contraction*. He goes on to say:

> *We experience expansion as awareness, comprehension, under-standing, or whatever we wish to call it.*

When we are completely expanded, we have a feeling of total awareness, of being one with all life. At that level we have no resistance to any vibrations or interactions with other beings. It is timeless bliss, with unlimited choice of consciousness, perception, and feeling.

On the other hand, a (human) being who is totally contracted is a mass particle, completely imploded.

To the degree that the person is contracted, that (human) being is unable to be in the same space with others, so contraction is felt as fear, pain, unconsciousness, ignorance, hatred, evil, and a whole host of strange feelings.

At an extreme (of contraction), a human being has the feeling of being completely insane, of resisting everyone and everything, of being unable to choose the content of consciousness.

Of course, these are just the feelings appropriate to mass vibration levels, and the person can get out of them at any time by expanding, by letting go of all resistance to what is thought, seen, or felt.

Stay with me here. Because what Golas says is profoundly important. When you're feeling oppressed, overwhelmed, exhausted by more than you can control—contracted, as Golas puts it—you can change your state to one of expansion.

According to Golas, the more contracted we are, the more threatened by change; the more expanded we are, the more open to change.

In our most enlightened—that is, open—state, change is as welcome as nonchange. Everything is perceived as a part of ourselves. There is no inside or outside. Everything is one thing. Our sense of isolation is transformed to a feeling of ease, of light, of joyful relationship with everything.

As infants, we didn't even think of change in the same way, because we lived those first days in an unthreatened state. Insensitive to the threat of loss, most young children are only aware of *what is*. Change is simply another form of *what is*. Change just *is*.

However, when we are in our most contracted—that is, closed—state, change is the most extreme threat. If the known is what I have, then the unknown must be what threatens to take away what I have. Change, then, is the unknown. And the unknown is fear. It's like being between trapezes.

To the fearful, change is threatening because things may get worse.

To the hopeful, change is encouraging because things may get better.

To the confident, change is inspiring because the challenge exists to improve things.

If you are fearful, you see difficulties in every opportunity. If you are fear-free, you see opportunities in every difficulty.

Fear protects what I have from being taken away. But it also disconnects me from the rest of the world. In other words, fear keeps me separate and alone.

Here's the exciting part of Golas's message: With this new understanding of contraction and expansion, we can become completely attuned to where we are at all times.

If I am afraid, suspicious, skeptical, and resistant, I am in a contracted state. If I am joyful, open, interested, and willing, I am in an expanded state. Just knowing this puts me on an expanded path. Always remembering this, Golas says, brings enlightenment, which opens me even more.

Such openness gives me the ability to access my options freely. And taking advantage of options is the best part of change. Just as there are infinite ways to greet a client, there are infinite ways to run your practice. If you believe Thaddeus Golas, your most exciting option is to be open to all of them.

Because your life is lived on a continuum between the most contracted and most expanded—the most closed and most open—states, change is best understood as the movement from one to the other, and back again.

Most small-business owners I've met see change as a thing-in-itself, as something that just happens to them. Most experience change as a threat. Whenever change shows up at the door, they quickly slam it. Many bolt the door and pile up the furniture. Some even run for their gun.

Few of them understand that change isn't a thing-in-itself, but rather the manifestation of many things. You might call it the revelation of all possibilities. Think of it as the ability at any moment to sacrifice what we are for what we could become.

Change can either challenge us or threaten us. It's our choice. Our attitude toward change can either pave the way to success or throw up a roadblock.

Change is where opportunity lives. Without change we would stay exactly as we are. The universe would be frozen still. Time would end.

At any given moment, we are somewhere on the path between a contracted and expanded state. Most of us are in the middle of the journey, neither totally closed nor totally open. According to Golas, change is our movement from one place in the middle toward one of the two ends.

Do you want to move toward contraction or toward enlightenment? Because without change, you are hopelessly stuck with what you've got.

Without change:

- We have no hope.
- We cannot know true joy.
- We will not get better.
- We will continue to focus exclusively on what we have and the threat of losing it.

All of this negativity contracts us even more, until, at the extreme closed end of the spectrum, we become a black hole so dense that no light can get in or out.

Sadly, the harder we try to hold on to what we've got, the less able we are to do so. So we try still harder, which eventually drags us even deeper into the black hole of contraction.

Are you like that? Do you know anybody who is?

Think of change as the movement between where we are and where we're not. That leaves only two directions for change: either moving forward or slipping backward. We either become more contracted or more expanded.

The next step is to link change to how we feel. If we feel afraid, change is dragging us backward. If we feel open, change is pushing us forward.

Change is not a thing-in-itself, but a movement of our consciousness. By tuning in, by paying attention, we get clues to the state of our being.

Change, then, is not an outcome or something to be acquired. Change is a shift of our consciousness, of our being, of our humanity, of our attention, of our relationship with all other beings in the universe.

We are either "more in relationship" or "less in relationship." Change is the movement in either of those directions. The exciting part is that *we possess the ability to decide which way we go . . . and to know in the moment which way we're moving*.

Closed, open . . . . Open, closed. Two directions in the universe. The choice is yours.

Do you see the profound opportunity available to you? What an extraordinary way to live!

Enlightenment is not reserved for the sainted. Rather, it comes to us as we become more sensitive to ourselves. Eventually, we become our own guides, alerting ourselves to our state, moment by moment: *Open . . . Closed . . . Open . . . Closed*.

Listen to your inner voice, your ally, and feel what it's like to be open and closed. Experience the instant of choice in both directions.

You will feel the awareness growing. It may be only a flash at first, so be alert. This feeling is accessible, but only if you avoid the black hole of contraction.

Are you afraid that you're totally contracted? Don't be—it's doubtful. The fact that you're still reading this book suggests that you're moving in the opposite direction.

You're more like a running-back seeking the open field. You can see the opportunity gleaming in the distance. In the open direction.

Understand that I'm not saying that change itself is a point on the path; rather, it's the all-important movement.

Change is *in you*, not *out there*.

What path are you on? The path of Liberation? Or the path of Crystallization?

As we know, change can be for the better or for the worse.

If change is happening *inside* of you, it is for the worse only if you remain closed to it. The key, then, is your attitude—your acceptance or rejection of change. Change can be for the better only if you accept it. And it will certainly be for the worse if you don't.

Remember, change is nothing in itself. Without you, change doesn't exist. Change is happening inside of each of us, giving us clues to where we are at any point in time.

Rejoice in change, for it's a sign you are alive.

Are we open? Are we closed? If we're open, good things are bound to happen. If we're closed, things will only get worse.

According to Golas, it's as simple as that. Whatever happens defines where we are. *How* we are is *where* we are. It cannot be any other way.

For change is life.

Charles Darwin taught that it is not the strongest of the species that survive, nor the most intelligent, but the one that proves itself most responsive to change.

The growth of your accounting practice, then, is its change. Your role is to go with it, be with it, share the joy, embrace the opportunities, meet the challenges, learn the lessons.

Remember, there are three kinds of people: (1) those who make things happen, (2) those who let things happen, and

(3) those who wonder what the hell happened. The people who make things happen are masters of change. The other two are its victims.

Which type are you?

The Big Change

If all this is going to mean anything to the life of your practice, you have to know when you're going to leave it. At what point, in your practice's rise from where it is now to where it can ultimately grow, are you going to sell it? Because if you don't have a clear picture of when you want out, your practice is the master of your destiny, not the reverse.

As we stated earlier, the most valuable form of money is equity, and unless your business vision includes your equity and how you will use it to your advantage, you will forever be consumed by your practice.

Your practice is potentially the best friend you ever had. It is your practice's nature to serve you, so let it. If, however, you are not a wise steward, if you do not tell your practice what you expect from it, it will run rampant, abuse you, use you, and confuse you.

Change. Growth. Equity.

Focus on the point in the future when you will take leave of your practice. Now reconsider your goals in that context. Be specific. Write them down.

Skipping this step is like tiptoeing through earthquake country. Who can say where the fault lies waiting? And who knows exactly when your whole world may come crashing down around you?

Which brings us to the subject of *time*. But first, let's listen to what Darren has to say about *change*.

CHAPTER 20

The Next Generation Accounting Firm

M. Darren Root

The question is not whether we are able to change but whether we are changing fast enough.

—Angela Merkel

The Next Generation Accounting Firm™ is a phrase I trademarked a few years ago. I've spent countless hours writing and speaking on this particular subject. My team has also developed a "Next Generation Accounting Firm" guide, which focuses on the need for accounting firms to embrace change in order to grow and prosper. At the core, a Next Generation Accounting Firm is about lifelong development—and for that, accountants must open their minds to change and the work that goes with it.

The accounting profession as a whole is rarely accused of being a group of early adopters, whether it's adoption of technology, processes, or best practices—a stereotype that, I admit, is well deserved. Accountants, inherently, are slow adopters, often waiting for others to test new technology or ideas first. To be an early adopter means to take a risk, and accountants naturally lean toward being cautious when faced with change.

Although the accounting profession may be slower to adopt change than others, the fact is that change does happen—and change has improved the working conditions in many firms. Think back a number of years and compare it to where the profession is today—much impressive change has occurred.

In the 1970s, accountants performed all processes manually. In the 1980s, firms embraced personal computers and electronic tax return preparation software. The 1990s brought mass adoption of desktop accounting software, a move toward digital audit processes, and the explosion of e-mail communication. In the 2000s, the buzz centered on software suites, multiple monitors, the paperless office and, of course, Internet technologies.

It's clear that change has happened over the years—more than most accountants realize. The real question, however, is not whether change has occurred, but rather, how quickly firms adapt to it. Are you among the laggards . . . always reluctant to change, fighting it every step of the way? If so, it's time to change your way of thinking. The faster accountants accept this, the easier the transition to next-generation status will be.

Here's the cold, hard truth: We are living in an on-demand world. E-mail hits our inbox, and clients expect an instant response. When clients request copies of tax returns be sent to a financial institution, they want them sent immediately. Like us, clients are busy, and as such they demand real-time, 24/7 access to their financial information—without calling, e-mailing, and waiting for a response. It's how the world operates. Think about it. No one would use a bank that didn't offer online services or a financial advisor who didn't provide immediate Web access to the client's financial portfolio.

And for those who still may cling to the notion that technology will make tax and accounting professionals obsolete, it's time to let that go as well. Our profession continues to be defined by technology. Take, for example, technology designed to help clients better operate their businesses. Desktop accounting software has been around for more than 20 years, and did it make accounting firms obsolete? Absolutely not. We've also seen the proliferation of individual income tax software for the do-it-yourselfers. But again, this proliferation has not truly affected the profession.

Now consider advanced technology for accounting firms. This technology is designed to improve workflow and elevate efficiency, which translates into enhanced services for our clients. For example, offering portals where clients can access and print their financial documents doesn't cut out the accountant; it improves the process for serving clients, which is what clients expect. Clients will still need their trusted advisor to ensure success.

Technology advances for the accounting profession are not slowing down. In fact, I would suggest they're speeding up. As executive editor of *The CPA Technology Advisor*, I have the opportunity to meet regularly with many technology vendors within the accounting space. In such meetings, I see an ongoing commitment to continually develop and enhance applications and services. The explosion of SaaS (Software as a Service) technology over the past few years is the best indication of how fast technology is changing. The focus is on helping firms operate more efficiently.

Running a successful firm requires advanced technology. View changes in technology as a positive thing, not as a curse.

These days, it's not uncommon to require between 7 and 10 different solutions to support a firm's processes. As applications evolve, accountants must be diligent and stay apprised of functionality. It's simply part of the commitment a business leader must make.

Many accountants I talk to are starting to realize that change is part of running their businesses. I think the challenge for most is not so much realizing they need to change and adapt, but rather developing an understanding of *how* to change. So many firm leaders simply don't know where to start. Such confusion leaves most practitioners stuck in the same place year after year—that is, doing it, doing it, doing it.

Change and Community Learning

When it comes to new technologies, accountants don't have to go it alone. Staying one step ahead of technology or practice trends can be a daunting challenge. So I advocate that firms get involved in something I call *community learning*. Community learning gets accountants out of the confines of their own firms and involved in groups that are focused on education and continued learning for the accounting profession. These groups consist of practicing accountants who all have the same goal of transitioning to next-generation status. Working together, practitioners share knowledge and form new ideas. Within noncompetitive community forums, accountants have access to a larger network of business leaders, sharing the onus of keeping up with change among a larger group. Community learning is a critical component of any firm's broad business plan.

For several years, I've personally led a series of community learning groups. Groups are made up of like-minded accounting professionals who come together to exchange information openly. I facilitate discussions centered on strategic firm direction, best practices, and process implementation. Through such events, I see the lightbulbs go on over participants' heads—that moment when they truly understand what is needed to implement change and move forward in growing their businesses. This is the central goal of community learning.

Change Means Opportunity

We've established that change is good. Change also means opportunity—the opportunity to grow, to learn, and to achieve new goals that you may not have thought possible. To take advantage of these opportunities, you will need to be open to the changes that are coming—changes that require you to rethink how you approach your practice. And isn't this what you really want for your firm? That is, the opportunity to be a leader, to set the pace, to lead your clients in the direction they should go? Of course it is. So the time has come to reengineer your practice into a business.

There is a lot to think about and a lot to do. And it won't all happen overnight. To implement change, you must put a strategic plan in place and follow through on it. Remember Chapter 6, where I talked about defining the business you want to be in, the services you want to offer, and how to deliver your vision? Once you've done the work defining who you are, it's time to write out the actions required to support your grand vision. These actions could include:

- Creating a place on your web site that supports online communication with your clients
- Identifying the technologies required to support a completely online payroll service offering
- Implementing video within your web site to market your firm, provide a brief welcome message to visitors, and provide

tutorials to clients on how to use their client portal, complete an online tax organizer, and so on

- Developing a blog for your home page that serves as a key information resource for your clients, including updates on tax laws, advice on long-term saving, and more

- Implementing a social media program, including creating a professional presence on Facebook, Twitter, and LinkedIn—and merging social media into your broad marketing program as another channel to connect and communicate with clients

- Identifying and joining appropriate community learning groups to stay apprised of change in the profession, including advances in technology and best practices

- Developing professional marketing collateral that represents your brand image and tells the right story about your firm and the services you offer

This list is certainly not all-inclusive, but you get the idea. It takes a lot of work to plan for your firm's success and identify the changes required to make that happen. I've always enjoyed the book *Who Moved My Cheese* by Spencer Johnson. In the accounting profession, like all other professions, the cheese is constantly being moved—that is, change happens. We can no longer rely on a "same as last year" mentality. Change will continue to come, and you have to be ready. Accepting that change is rapid and perpetual is the first big step in becoming a Next Generation Accounting Firm.

CHAPTER 21

On the Subject of Time

Michael E. Gerber

Take time to deliberate; but when the time for action arrives, stop thinking and go in.

—Andrew Jackson

"I'm running out of time!" accountants often lament. "I've got to learn how to manage my time more carefully!"

Of course, they see no real solution to this problem. They're just worrying the subject to death. Singing the accountant's blues.

Some make a real effort to control time. Maybe they go to time management classes or faithfully try to record their activities during every hour of the day.

But it's hopeless. Even when accountants work harder, even when they keep precise records of their time, there's always a shortage of it. It's as if they're looking at a square clock in a round

143

universe. Something doesn't fit. The result: The accountant is constantly chasing work, money, life.

And the reason is simple. Accountants don't see time for what it really is. They think of time with a small *t*, rather than Time with a capital *T*.

Yet Time is simply another word for *your life*. It's your ultimate asset, your gift at birth—and you can spend it any way you want. Do you know how you want to spend it? Do you have a plan?

How do *you* deal with Time? Are you even conscious of it? If you are, I bet you are constantly locked into either the future or the past. Relying on either memory or imagination.

Do you recognize these voices? "Once I get through this, I can have a drink . . . go on a vacation . . . retire." "I remember when I was young and practicing accounting was satisfying."

As you go to bed at midnight, are you thinking about waking up at 7 A.M. so that you can get to the office by 8 A.M. so that you can go to lunch by noon, because your software people will be there at 1:30 P.M. and you've got a full schedule and a new client scheduled at 2:30?

Most of us are prisoners of the future or the past. While pinballing between the two, we miss the richest moments of our life—the present. Trapped forever in memory or imagination, we are strangers to the here and now. Our future is nothing more than an extension of our past, and the present is merely the background.

It's sobering to think that right now each of us is at a precise spot somewhere between the beginning of our Time (our birth) and the end of our Time (our death).

No wonder everyone frets about Time. What really terrifies us is that *we're using up our life and we can't stop it*.

It feels as if we're plummeting toward the end with nothing to break our free fall. Time is out of control! Understandably, this is horrifying, mostly because the real issue is not time with a small *t* but Death with a big *D*.

From the depths of our existential anxiety, we try to put Time in a different perspective—all the while pretending we can manage it. We talk about Time as though it were something other than what it is. "Time is money," we announce, as though that explains it.

But what every accountant should know is that Time is life. And Time ends! Life ends!

The big, walloping, irresolvable problem is that *we don't know how much Time we have left.*

Do you feel the fear? Do you want to get over it?

Let's look at Time more seriously.

To fully grasp Time with a capital *T*, you have to ask the Big Question: *How do I wish to spend the rest of my Time?*

Because I can assure you that if you don't ask that Big Question with a big *Q*, you will forever be assailed by the little questions. You'll shrink the whole of your life to *this time* and *next time* and the *last time*—all the while wondering, *What time is it?*

It's like running around the deck of a sinking ship worrying about where you left the keys to your cabin.

You must accept that you have only so much Time; that you're using up that Time second by precious second. And that your Time, your life, is the most valuable asset you have. Of course, you can use your Time any way you want. But unless you choose to use it as richly, as rewardingly, as excitingly, as intelligently, as *intentionally* as possible, you'll squander it and fail to appreciate it.

Indeed, if you are oblivious to the value of your Time, you'll commit the single greatest sin: You will live your life unconscious of its passing you by.

Until you deal with Time with a capital *T*, you'll worry about time with a small *t* until you have no Time—or life—left. Then your Time will be history . . . along with your life.

I can anticipate the question: If Time is the problem, why not just take on fewer clients? Well, that's certainly an option, but probably not necessary. I know an accountant with a small practice who sees four times as many clients as the average, yet he doesn't work long hours. How is it possible?

This accountant has a system. By using this expert system, the employees can do everything the accountant or his associate accountants would do—everything that isn't accountant-dependent.

Be versus Do

Remember when we all asked, "What do I want to be when I grow up?" It was one of our biggest concerns as children.

Notice that the question isn't, "What do I want to *do* when I grow up?" It's "What do I want to *be?*"

Shakespeare wrote, "To be or not to be." Not, "To do or not to do."

But when you grow up, people always ask you, "What do you *do?*" How did the question change from *being* to *doing?* How did we miss the critical distinction between the two?

Even as children, we sensed the distinction. The real question we were asking was not what we would end up *doing* when we grew up, but who we would *be*.

We were talking about a *life* choice, not a *work* choice. We instinctively saw it as a matter of how we spend our Time, not what we do *in* time.

Look to children for guidance. I believe that as children we instinctively saw Time as life and tried to use it wisely. As children, we wanted to make a life choice, not a work choice. As children, we didn't know—or care—that work had to be done on time, on budget.

Until you see Time for what it really is—your life span—you will always ask the wrong question.

Until you embrace the whole of your Time and shape it accordingly, you will never be able to fully appreciate the moment.

Until you fully appreciate every second that comprises Time, you will never be sufficiently motivated to live those seconds fully.

Until you're sufficiently motivated to live those seconds fully, you will never see fit to change the way you are. You will never take the quality and sanctity of Time seriously.

And unless you take the sanctity of Time seriously, you will continue to struggle to catch up with something behind you. Your frustrations will mount as you try to snatch the second that just whisked by.

If you constantly fret about time with a small *t*, then big-*T* Time will blow right past you. And you'll miss the whole point, the real truth about Time: You can't manage it; you never could. You can only *live* it.

And so that leaves you with these questions: How do I live my life? How do I give significance to it? How can I be here now, in this moment?

Once you begin to ask these questions, you'll find yourself moving toward a much fuller, richer life. But if you continue to be caught up in the banal work you do every day, you're never going to find the time to take a deep breath, exhale, and be present in the now.

So, let's talk about the subject of *work*. But first, let's listen to what Darren has to say about *time*.

CHAPTER 22

Managing Choices, Not Time

M. Darren Root

*Time is free, but it's priceless. You can't own it, but you can use it.
You can't keep it, but you can spend it. Once you've lost it, you can
never get it back.*

—Harvey Mackay

Apple Chief Executive Officer (CEO), Steve Jobs, has long
been one of my favorite business leaders. I appreciate the
creativity, design, and vision that he infuses in everything
Apple. I also like his perspective on the subject of time. Jobs (n.d.)
stated:

Your time is limited, so don't waste it living someone else's life. Don't be trapped by dogma, which is living with the results of other people's thinking. Don't let the noise of others' opinions drown out your own inner voice. And most important, have the courage to follow your heart and intuition. They somehow already know what you truly want to become. Everything else is secondary. (Retrieved from: http://thinkexist.com/quotes/steve_jobs)

Certain expectations about time and schedule have long pervaded the accounting profession. Due to the nature of deadlines and workload compression, accountants always seem to be on the same crazy path, working long, exhausting hours. I have witnessed many people enter the profession, experience a single chaotic season, and then decide that accounting is not for them. This is unfortunate, because we have it within our power to create the business we desire . . . one without oppressive work schedules.

In Chapter 21, Michael teaches us that time and life are essentially synonymous: The *time* you have left is really the *life* you have left. I believe this is true, which is why I continually promote creating true life–work balance in my presentations, articles, and web casts. Next Generation Accounting Firms understand the necessity of balancing work with personal pursuits and strive to implement the necessary technologies and processes to ensure this balance. Leaders behind next-generation firms know that time is limited and treat it as a precious commodity.

If you are tired of living the life of the traditional accounting-firm model, you *can* do something about it. First, it's all about making a choice. Think about the following questions:

- Do you want to work your life away?
- Do you want to adhere to other people's ways of thinking, or do you want to break free of outdated popular opinion and forge your own path?

- Do you want a life that is balanced—one that allows you to spend time with your kids, travel with your family, and engage in new and exciting adventures with your spouse?

You know what you want; otherwise you would not be reading this book. Now is the time to listen to your own inner voice and follow your heart and intuition . . . because everything else really is secondary! Once you've decided to create balance between work and life, the next step is understanding the difference between managing your time and managing your choices.

Time versus Choices

Michael says, "We can't really manage time." In other words, we need to manage our choices, not the minutes in each day.

In *The 7 Habits of Highly Effective People*, Stephen R. Covey talks about forming positive habits to aid in making better choices. Habit 1 is to *Be Proactive*, which means *you* choose your path. It's that simple; you are the engineer of your life, so you are the one who chooses your path and your destination. Habit 2 is to *Put First Things First*. This directs you to identify your "big rocks," that is the things in your life that are most important, and put them first. By uncovering your big rocks, you create an initial checklist of what you need to accomplish.

I've also long been a student of Dan Sullivan, following his program The Strategic Coach. At the center of his message is a call to figure out the areas where you excel and then spend most your time on those activities. For example, if your strengths are strategic planning and education, you should be spending most of your time facilitating these activities. In the same vein, you should reallocate activities that fall outside your areas of strength. If you struggle with writing, for example, you would not put yourself in charge of proposal or engagement-letter development;

instead, you'd farm out writing tasks to a staff member with strong written communication skills. Again, it's about managing your choices.

How you handle the volumes of information coming into your firm is another important choice you will make as you strive for life–work balance. Again, you can choose to continue to do things the old way, or you can open yourself up to a new way.

Technology, for all its benefits, has created a significant number of challenges for accountants. E-mail is a good example. Like me, no doubt you deal with "e-mail flooding"—the constant flow of e-mails into your inbox. It never seems to stop. And with the proliferation of mobile devices, you can't escape the perpetual inflow of digital communications. On top of this, there's also the continuous inflow of client data, contact information, the need to maintain an updated schedule, and on and on.

What do you do? Here's a better question: What choices do you make to ensure you are operating at peak efficiency *and* leaving ample time for a personal life?

The first step is to analyze your current situation. How are you spending your days? Are some tasks better handled by administrative staff—whether it's paying bills, making deposits, scheduling your appointments, or meeting with clients to obtain signatures on documents? Make a detailed analysis of your daily activity to identify tasks you can reallocate, freeing you so you can easily keep up with communications and get out of the office now and then.

Once you have thoroughly analyzed how you spend your time and delegated activities appropriately among your staff, you will be better equipped to plan how you spend your time going forward.

Personally, I have found that planning time in week intervals is most effective. When you look at your week, first schedule your "big rocks." All other activities will fall into place, including exercise, relaxation, and recreation. It's good practice to schedule small blocks of time each day for answering communications. You'll be surprised at how easy it is to keep up with e-mail, voice mail, and other digital messages when you allot just 15 to 30 minutes a day to the task.

A methodical process for blocking your time also allows you to schedule regular meetings for strategic planning and staff training. And it really is about being strategic. For example, your firm is far more likely to succeed when you spend your time on your big rocks, as opposed to answering e-mails all day long.

Using Technology to Your Advantage

Be sure to use technology to your advantage. All too often, I see accountants scheduling on-site appointments as a primary means for client interaction. I understand the necessity of meeting face-to-face; it creates intimacy and a bond between clients and their trusted advisor. However, accountants often schedule unnecessary on-site appointments. Remember, your clients are just as busy as you are, so often they'll appreciate online communications over an on-site meeting. Communicating online is fast and convenient, and it doesn't interrupt daily operations.

Today, most clients expect online services, so take advantage of that expectation. Clients appreciate getting an e-mail alert that documents are ready for review and being able to access those documents within an online portal. Don't think you are short-changing the client by relying heavily on technology to communicate; they rely on it, too!

You should also use technology to communicate internally with staff. Digital communication is a reliable vehicle for transferring knowledge and up-to-date information. Many of today's applications can capture volumes of information, allowing staff to consult technology to make decisions, and not run every detail by you personally. Empower your staff to make decisions, and watch how your availability goes through the roof.

The fact is that most interruptions within a firm's daily operations come from within. That is, we create the interruptions via our own bad choices. We set the wrong expectations with clients and staff; we don't use technology to our advantage; we haven't defined our areas of greatness; we don't follow our intuition and heart. All this adds up to wasted time.

The suggestions in this chapter will help you begin to get a handle on your workday. No single idea is a magic bullet to solve all your issues. You will need to conduct the proper analysis of your own situation and make the right choices to get on the path to true life–work balance.

CHAPTER 23

On the Subject of Work

Michael E. Gerber

As we learn we always change, and so does our perception. This changed perception then becomes a new Teacher inside each of us.
—Hyemeyohsts Storm

In the business world, as the saying goes, the entrepreneur knows something about everything, the technician knows everything about something, and the switchboard operator just knows everything.

In an accounting practice, accountants see their natural work as the work of the technician. The supreme technician. Often to the exclusion of everything else.

After all, accountants get zero preparation working as a manager and spend no time thinking as an entrepreneur—those just aren't courses offered in today's schools and colleges of accounting. By the time they own their own accounting practice, they're just doing it, doing it, doing it.

At the same time, they want everything—freedom, respect, money. Most of all, they want to rid themselves of meddling bosses and start their own practice. That way, they can be their own boss and take home all the money. These accountants are in the throes of an entrepreneurial seizure.

Accountants who have been praised for their ability to resolve difficult tax cases or their extensive knowledge of accounting systems believe they have what it takes to run an accounting practice. It's not unlike the plumber who becomes a contractor because he's a great plumber. Sure, he may be a great plumber . . . but it doesn't necessarily follow that he knows how to build a practice that does this work.

It's the same for an accountant. So many of them are surprised to wake up one morning and discover that they're nowhere near as equipped for owning their own practice as they thought they were.

More than any other subject, work is the cause of obsessive-compulsive behavior by accountants.

Work. You've got to do it every single day.

Work. If you fall behind, you'll pay for it.

Work. There's either too much or not enough.

So many accountants describe work as what they do when they're busy. Some discriminate between the work they *could* be doing as accountants and the work they *should* be doing as accountants.

But according to the E-Myth, they're exactly the same thing. The work you *could* do and the work you *should* do as an accountant are identical. Let me explain.

Strategic Work versus Tactical Work

Accountants can do only two kinds of work: strategic work and tactical work.

Tactical work is easier to understand, because it's what almost every accountant does almost every minute of every hour of every day. It's called getting the job done. It's called doing business.

Tactical work includes filing, billing, answering the telephone, going to the bank, and seeing clients.

The E-Myth says that tactical work is all the work accountants find themselves doing in an accounting practice to *avoid* doing the strategic work.

"I'm too busy," most accountants will tell you.

"How come nothing goes right unless I do it myself?" they complain in frustration.

Accountants say these things when they're up to their ears in tactical work. But most accountants don't understand that if they had done more strategic work, they would have less tactical work to do.

Accountants are doing strategic work when they ask the following questions:

- Why am I an accountant?
- What will my practice look like when it's done?
- What must my practice look, act, and feel like in order for it to compete successfully?
- How do I define success in my practice?

Please note that I said accountants *ask* these questions when they are doing strategic work. I didn't say these are the questions they necessarily answer.

That is the fundamental difference between strategic work and tactical work. Tactical work is all about *answers:* How to do this. How to do that.

Strategic work, in contrast, is all about *questions:* What practice are we really in? Why are we in that practice? Who specifically is our practice determined to serve? When will I sell this practice? How and where will this practice be doing business when I sell it? And so forth.

Not that strategic questions don't have answers. Accountants who commonly ask strategic questions know that once they ask such a question, they're already on their way to *envisioning* the answer. Question and answer are part of a whole. You can't find the right answer until you've asked the right question.

Tactical work is much easier, because the question is always more obvious. In fact, you don't ask the tactical question; instead, the question arises from a result you need to get or a problem you need to solve. Billing a client is tactical work. Filing a return is tactical work. Firing an employee is tactical work. Performing an audit is tactical work.

Tactical work is the stuff you do every day in your practice. Strategic work is the stuff you plan to do to create an exceptional practice/business/enterprise.

In tactical work, the question comes from *out there* rather than *in here*. The tactical question is about something *outside* of you, whereas the strategic question is about something *inside* of you.

The tactical question is about something you *need* to do, whereas the strategic question is about something you *want* to do. Want versus need.

If tactical work consumes you:

- You are always reacting to something outside of you.
- Your practice runs you; you don't run it.

- Your employees run you; you don't run them.
- Your life runs you; you don't run your life.

You must understand that the more strategic work you do, the more intentional your decisions, your practice, and your life become. *Intention* is the byword of strategic work.

Everything on the outside begins to serve you, to serve your vision, rather than forcing you to serve it. Everything you *need* to do is congruent with what you *want* to do. It means you have a vision, an aim, a purpose, a strategy, an *envisioned* result.

Strategic work is the work you do to *design* your practice, to design your life.

Tactical work is the work you do to *implement* the design created by strategic work.

Without strategic work, there is no design. Without strategic work, all that's left is keeping busy.

There's only one thing left to do. It's time to take action. But first, let's listen to what Darren has to say on the subject of *work*.

CHAPTER 24

Getting to the Real Work

M. Darren Root

I put all my genius into my life; I put only my talents into my works.
—Oscar Wilde

B y our very nature, accountants are technicians. As a profession, we define our work around our skills and our ability to perform those skills. We are tax and accounting professionals; therefore, our work neatly comprises all tasks associated with preparing and processing financials.

But that's simply not true.

We are accountants; that is a fact. However, our talents range far beyond our technical skills in preparing tax returns and financial statements. We are creative leaders, marketers, strategists, and planning sages. If we weren't, we would not own a business in the first place. The trick is to tap into these talents, embrace them—and let loose.

One of the most difficult tasks I face in working with accountants is changing the narrow perception that our talents are limited to technical tasks. An even bigger challenge is trying to instill an understanding that strategy, planning, educating, and leading also fall under the broad work umbrella. If you've implemented the appropriate systems and processes, your well-trained staff can easily and competently handle important client work. This allows you, the firm's leader, to focus on your most important job. You guessed it: Leading!

Savvy business leaders have mastered the art of strategic planning to lead their firms in a positive direction. Dedicated planning and focused strategies are what will change your business in a significant way; preparation of tax returns or processing payroll will not. If your days are filled with technician work, along with responding to e-mails and meeting with clients, you don't stand a chance in moving beyond technician status.

What is it about the profession that leads us to a mentality of "If I don't do it, it won't get done properly"? I see this more and more in my travels. The irony here is that I meet accountants through my Next Generation Accounting Firm summits. Clearly, just by being there, the accountants who attend are open to a new way of doing business, yet they still cling to an old way of thinking.

I'm not sure why accountants are pulled so strongly to the technician side. I only know that their attitudes must change. And change often comes when we better understand how we came to be in the position we are in—the position of working "in" our firms, constantly buried by daily administrative tasks.

I've approached the issue with an academic mind-set. Over the past few years I've spoken to hundreds of accounts to conduct my own qualitative study. As I interview participants within my sample group, over and over I hear, "I'm too busy to implement the ideas you offer." In return I ask, "How do you spend your day?" The following are the most common responses:

- Resolving information technology (IT) issues
- Meeting with clients
- Setting up new clients
- Returning phone calls and e-mails
- Scheduling appointments
- Preparing tax returns
- Preparing financial statements

Does this sound like a typical day for you? If you answered, "Yes," my reply is: "Stop!"

As I mentioned in Chapter 22, you must identify your personal areas of greatness and focus on performing those tasks while delegating the others. The majority of tasks that accountants said they perform daily are things that can easily be reallocated to staff, whether to professional staff or administrative employees. There is no reason why, as the leader of your firm, you should be meeting with clients all day, dealing with IT issues, or scheduling appointments. Build the right team, train appropriately, and start to delegate these tasks—today!

I've found that there is no greater motivator than assigning new and challenging responsibilities. If you have the right staff on the bus, they will eagerly accept new tasks and view them as a learning experience and an opportunity to grow within the firm. Those who scoff at new responsibilities shouldn't be on your bus in the first place. Allow your staff to engage with clients and operate as a valued component within your system—and then sit back and watch the work get done. Watch your free time increase—time you can dedicate to strategy and planning.

As an example, take a moment to consider the process within a completely different professional system. You have an appointment with your optometrist. You check in with reception, where the receptionist captures your basic information. You are then escorted to a room where a technician tests your visual acuity and runs glaucoma, eye movement, and focusing tests. Finally, the optometrist enters to perform more intricate tests and provide a complete eye evaluation. When the optometrist is done, your chart goes back to the technician to schedule a follow-up visit or support you in selecting eyeglass frames.

You see where I am going, right? The optometrist spends maybe 20 minutes with you in total. All other components of the appointment are allocated to qualified staff. This allows the optometrist to concentrate on patient care and provide informed feedback. But wait, there's a bigger point here. Even though you've spent little time with the doctor, do you feel you received lower-quality service? Of course not—and neither will your clients.

Part of operating a Next Generation Accounting Firm is creating a new set of expectations among your clients. Just as a patient expects to see more of the nurse than the doctor during a routine office visit; your clients need to be conditioned to work more with your very competent staff and less with you. Like at the doctor's office; this should be a completely acceptable experience. You can accomplish this over time as you reengineer your internal systems and allow your staff to be active participants in serving your client base. As long as clients' needs are met, they will not care whether they see you to sign their tax return or your administrative assistant.

Understanding your role as the strategic leader of your business will change the way you define your work and the way your business operates. In Chapter 23, Michael notes that tactical work is all about answers and strategic work is all about questions. If you typically spend each day working tactically, it stands to reason that tomorrow you will work the very same way.

Begin to view yourself as the leader of your firm, ready to make changes and operate on a whole new level. This requires you to do the strategic work and ask the right questions. You can begin by asking:

- What processes are in place to accomplish each service offering?
- What processes are in place to accomplish daily operational tasks?
- What can I do to standardize processes firmwide, so everyone is performing every service and task uniformly?
- Are the right technologies in place to support execution of services and daily operational tasks?
- Can workflows be enhanced to execute services and tasks more effectively?
- Have we identified each obstacle in the process, whether for staff or clients, and have these obstacles been resolved?
- Have the appropriate staff members been identified and assigned to execute tasks within each process?
- Have all staff been properly trained to execute services and tasks within each process, including training for workflow activities and supporting technologies?

This list provides a good starting point to begin leading your firm in the right direction. It also serves to help you evaluate where you are currently, which will provide you with a clear picture of how much work you need to do.

Remember: Just because you've always done things in a certain way doesn't mean you have to continue that tradition. If it's not working, it's not working. Abandon the old and make way for the new. Create a strategic vision of your firm, taking the time to write down the details of where you see your business going. And with that very clear vision in mind, begin to design the business of your dreams.

CHAPTER 25

On the Subject of Taking Action

Michael E. Gerber

Deliberation is the work of many men. Action, of one alone.
—Charles de Gaulle

I t's time to get started, time to take action. Time to stop thinking about the old practice and start thinking about the new practice. It's not a matter of coming up with better practices; it's about reinventing the practice of accounting.

And the accountant has to take personal responsibility for it. That's you.

So sit up and pay attention!

You, the accountant, have to be interested. You cannot abdicate accountability for the practice of accounting, the administration of accounting, or the financial life of your accounting practice.

Although the goal is to create systems into which accountants can plug reasonably competent people—systems that allow the practice to run without them—accountants must take responsibility for that happening.

I can hear the chorus now: "But we're accountants! We shouldn't have to know about this." To that I say: whatever. If you don't give a flip about your practice, fine—close your mind to new knowledge and accountability. But if you want to succeed, then you'd better step up and take responsibility, and you'd better do it now.

All too often, accountants take no responsibility for the business of accounting but instead delegate tasks without any understanding of what it takes to do them; without any interest in what their people are actually doing; without any sense of what it feels like to be at the front desk when a client comes in and has to wait for 45 minutes; and without any appreciation for the entity that is creating their livelihood.

Accountants can open the portals of change in an instant. All you have to do is say, "I don't want to do it that way anymore." Saying it will begin to set you free—even though you don't yet understand what the practice will look like after it's been reinvented.

This demands an intentional leap from the known into the unknown. It further demands that you live there—in the unknown—for a while. It means discarding the past, everything you once believed to be true.

Think of it as soaring rather than plunging.

Thought Control

You should by now be clear about the need to organize your thoughts first, then your business. Because the organization of your thoughts is the foundation for the organization of your business.

If we try to organize our business without organizing our thoughts, we will fail to attack the problem.

We have seen that organization is not simply time management. Nor is it people management. Nor is it tidying up desks or alphabetizing client files. Organization is first, last, and always cleaning up the mess of our minds.

By learning how to *think* about the practice of accounting, by learning how to *think* about your priorities, and by learning how to *think* about your life, you'll prepare yourself to do righteous battle with the forces of failure.

Right thinking leads to right action—and now is the time to take action. Because it is only through action that you can translate thoughts into movement in the real world, and, in the process, find fulfillment.

So, first, *think* about what you want to do. Then *do* it. Only in this way will you be fulfilled.

How do you put the principles we've discussed in this book to work in your accounting practice?

To find out, accompany me down the path once more:

1. *Create a story about your practice.* Your story should be an idealized version of your accounting practice, a vision of what the preeminent accountant in your field should be and why. Your story must become the very heart of your practice. It must become the spirit that mobilizes it, as well as everyone who walks through the doors. Without this story, your practice will be reduced to plain work.

2. *Organize your practice so that it breathes life into your story.* Unless your practice can faithfully replicate your story in action, it all becomes fiction. In that case, you'd be better off not telling your story at all. And without a story, you'd

be better off leaving your practice the way it is and just hoping for the best.

Here are some tips for organizing your accounting practice:

- Identify the key functions of your practice
- Identify the essential processes that link those functions
- Identify the results you have determined your practice will produce
- Clearly state in writing how each phase will work

Take it step by step. Think of your practice as a program, a piece of software, a system. It is a collaboration, a collection of processes dynamically interacting with one another.

Of course, your practice is also people.

Engage your people in the process.

Why is this the third step rather than the first? Because, contrary to the advice most business experts will give you, you must never engage your people in the process until you, yourself, are clear about what you intend to do.

The need for consensus is a disease of today's addled mind. It's a product of our troubled and confused times. When people don't know what to believe in, they often ask others to tell them. To ask is not to lead but to follow.

The prerequisite of sound leadership is first to know where you wish to go.

And so, "What do I want?" becomes the first question; not, "What do they want?" In your own practice, the vision must first be yours. To follow another's vision is to abdicate your personal accountability, your leadership role, your true power.

In short, the role of leader cannot be delegated or shared. And without leadership, no accounting practice will ever succeed.

Despite what you have been told, win-win is a secondary step, not a primary one. The opposite of win-win is not necessarily "they lose."

Let's say "they" can win by choosing a good horse. The best choice will not be made by consensus. "Guys, what horse do you think we should ride?" will always lead to endless and worthless discussions. By the time you're done jawing, the horse will have already left the post.

Before you talk to your people about what you intend to do in your practice and why you intend to do it, you need to reach agreement with yourself.

It's important to know (1) exactly what you want, (2) how you intend to proceed, (3) what's important to you and what isn't, and (4) what you want the practice to be and how you want it to get there.

Once you have that agreement, it's crucial that you engage your people in a discussion about what you intend to do and why. Be clear—both with yourself and with them.

The Story

The story is paramount because it is your vision. Tell it with passion and conviction. Tell it with precision. Never hurry a great story. Unveil it slowly. Don't mumble or show embarrassment. Never apologize or display false modesty. Look your audience in the eyes and tell your story as though it is the most important one they'll ever hear about business. Your business. The business into which you intend to pour your heart, your soul, your intelligence, your imagination, your time, your money, and your sweaty persistence.

Get into the storytelling zone. Behave as though it means everything to you. Show no equivocation when telling your story.

These tips are important because you're going to tell your story over and over—to clients, to new and old employees, to accountants, to associate accountants, and to your family and friends. You're going to tell it at your church or synagogue; to your card-playing or fishing buddies; and to organizations such as Kiwanis, Rotary, YMCA, Hadassah, and Boy Scouts.

There are few moments in your life when telling a great story about a great business is inappropriate.

If it is to be persuasive, you must love your story. Do you think Walt Disney loved his Disneyland story? Or Ray Kroc his McDonald's story? What about Fred Smith at Federal Express? Or Debbie Fields at Mrs. Field's Cookies? Or Tom Watson Jr. at IBM?

Do you think these people loved their stories? Do you think others loved (and *still* love) to hear them? I dare say *all* successful entrepreneurs have loved the story of their business. Because that's what true entrepreneurs do: They tell stories that come to life in the form of their business.

Remember: A great story never fails. A great story is always a joy to hear.

In summary, you first need to clarify, both for yourself and for your people, the *story* of your practice. Then you need to detail the *process* your practice must go through to make your story become reality.

I call this the business development process. Others call it reengineering, continuous improvement, reinventing your practice, or total quality management.

Whatever you call it, you must take three distinct steps to succeed:

1. *Innovation.* Continue to find better ways of doing what you do.
2. *Quantification.* Once that is achieved, quantify the impact of these improvements on your practice.

3. *Orchestration.* Once these improvements are verified, orchestrate this better way of running your practice so that it becomes your standard, to be repeated time and again.

In this way, the system works—no matter who's using it. And you've built a practice that works consistently, predictably, systematically. A practice you can depend on to operate exactly as promised, every single time.

Your vision, your people, your process—all linked.

A superior accounting practice is a creation of your imagination, a product of your mind. So fire it up and get started! Now let's listen to what Darren has to say about *taking action*.

CHAPTER
26

Getting Things Done

M. Darren Root

The secret to getting things done is to act.

—Dante Alighieri

"Getting it done" means different things to different people. I've met so many practitioners who indicate that they want to transition their firm into a business . . . to move from supreme technician to entrepreneur. They attend conference after conference in search of answers. Unfortunately, that is where "getting it done" ends. They seek out the information, but nothing ever changes.

It's time that you redefined what it means to get it done so you can invent the business you've always wanted.

Imagine a business where there is a system and process for every service and task, a business where your service offerings are

175

clearly defined and your staff members have the technical competence to execute each.

Let's keep going . . . .

Imagine a business where you have a technologically advanced web site that supports real-time client interaction, agency-level marketing materials, targeted e-mail campaigns, and a social media presence that attracts the right clientele. You have a support team that onboards new clients seamlessly from initial contact to implementation into the firm's standardized workflow. You have a business where staff and clients collaborate in real time using advanced technologies, where you spend the entire workday performing tasks you enjoy within your areas of greatness.

Sounds great, right?

Then go for it. The business I'm describing is completely within your reach. And the only obstacle in sight is you. Within this book, Michael has systematically provided you with the foundation to create your ideal business. Additionally, I have supplied you with insight, tested and proven strategies, and a detailed account of my own journey from an accounting technician to business leader. The time has come for you to act.

As I've said throughout the book, you must start with a strategic vision. Your vision needs to be exact and in writing. Establish your own big picture, define your big rocks, and identify your priorities.

No one is saying that this is an easy undertaking. You will most certainly need help to get started and periodically along the way. In my "Next Generation Accounting Firm" guide, I offer a simple formula: define, communicate, deliver. This formula provides a logical road map to help firms begin their move to next-generation status. Consider each step:

1. *Define* who you are.
2. *Communicate* with consistency and professionalism.
3. *Deliver* what you promise.

Define Who You Are

What is it you do best? What are your core competencies? What drives your economic engine? Every firm has areas of expertise; once you define yours, you can begin to capitalize on your strengths. For example, you should define:

- The niches you will serve
- The services you will offer
- The type of client you want to attract
- Your annual revenue goals
- How you will deliver services
- Your schedule—how many days per week you want to work

Once you have defined who you are, it is much easier to communicate your services clearly to clients and prospects and set up the processes to support the services you offer.

Communicate with Consistency and Professionalism

With every interaction, you communicate a message to clients and prospects. It's critical to ensure that you are always putting your best foot forward; one wrong communication can affect your overall image or attract the wrong type of client. You must consider each and every communication that takes place within your firm, including:

- The exterior and interior of your office
- Signage
- Your web site and social media presence
- Marketing collateral and e-campaigns
- Reception greeting

- Incoming call greeting
- Outgoing voice mail messages
- Business cards
- Stationery
- Premium giveaways

Your communication must be professional and consistent across the board; otherwise, your credibility is threatened.

Deliver What You Promise

If you communicate to clients that you are a technology-driven firm, you must deliver. Smart application of technology enables you to offer online, real-time services to clients and operate at peak efficiency. To develop a highly efficient delivery platform, consider the following issues:

- What software is in place: integrated suite or disparate components
- How technologies are integrated to obtain the highest level of efficiency and streamlined workflow processes
- Whether staff is properly trained and embraces the technologies in place

I developed the Next Generation Accounting Firm concept and the define, communicate, deliver formula as a result of reading *The E-Myth* more than 10 years ago. I absorbed and embraced Michael's philosophies—but more important, I took action.

In order to take action, you must first step away from your daily routine of doing it, doing it, doing it. This should be a regularly scheduled departure over an appropriate amount of time. Separation from daily tasks is the only way you can begin to plan and strategize.

In my consulting business, RootWorks, we have a saying: "A firm in motion stays in motion." The philosophy behind this phrase is that next-generation firms are ever active and vigilant— dedicated to research, education, planning, and strategic action. They are consistently in motion.

Getting your firm in motion is hard work. Don't expect to spend a few hours a day over the course of a few weeks. You need to be all-in and commit to creating your strategic vision and defining your big rocks—and these items take time. Once you start to get some momentum, you can then bring other key stakeholders within the firm into the process. However, getting things moving initially is completely up to you.

It's important to recognize clients and your staff in this transition, because once your transition begins there is no stopping.

If you already have a sound client base, which you probably do, you will need to transition your practice systematically. Once you have implemented necessary systems and processes, each new client who enters your firm should enter based on your new model. There will also be the low-hanging fruit in your existing client base, which can be transitioned fairly quickly, as well. You will have some legacy clients who may resist change, but be persistent.

You will also have staff members who show some resistance to change. Start by providing every staff member with a copy of this book, and ask them to read it carefully in preparation for a firm retreat. Use the retreat as a forum for emphasizing the philosophies within the book and helping staff understand the big picture. It is critical to get staff on board if you plan to stay in motion. Keeping them informed throughout the process is the best way to get them on board and have them stay there.

Trust me when I tell you that working hard on your business and witnessing the progress is energizing. It's the experience of the transformation itself that will keep you passionate and looking forward to each new day in the office. And feeling a true passion for work is like not working at all.

I am confident that if you follow these principles you will get there, and I am here to help. Contact us any time via our web site at www.michaelegerber.com/accountant.

AFTERWORD

For over three decades, I've applied the E-Myth principles I've shared with you here to the successful development of thousands of small businesses throughout the world. Many have been accounting practices—from small companies to large corporations, with accountants specializing in every field from public accounting to bookkeeping. Few rewards are greater than seeing these E-Myth principles improve the work and lives of so many people. Those rewards include seeing these changes:

- Lack of clarity—clarified
- Lack of organization—organized
- Lack of direction—shaped into a path that is clearly, lovingly, passionately pursued
- Lack of money or money poorly managed—money understood instead of coveted; created instead of chased; wisely spent or invested instead of squandered
- Lack of committed people—transformed into a cohesive community working in harmony toward a common goal; discovering each other and themselves in the process; all

the while expanding their understanding, their know-how, their interest, their attention

After working with so many accountants, I know that a practice can be much more than what most become. I also know that nothing is preventing you from making your practice all that it can be. It takes only desire and the perseverance to see it through.

In this book—the second of its kind in the new E-Myth Vertical series—the E-Myth principles have been complemented and enriched by stories from real-life accountants who have put these principles to use in their practice. These accountants, who have followed the guidance of my co-author, Darren Root, have had the desire and perseverance to achieve success beyond their wildest dreams. Now you, too, can join their ranks and place your Accounting practice on the highest possible professional level.

I hope this book has helped you clear your vision and set your sights on a very bright future.

To take action now, please contact us at www.michaele gerber.com/accountant.

To your practice and your life, good growing!